Mailboxes

20 unique step-by-step projects

Edited by
G.E.Novak

A Storey Publishing Book

STOREY

D1366473

Storey Communications, Inc.

The mission of Storey Communications is to serve our customers
by publishing practical information that encourages personal independence
in harmony with the environment.

Copyediting and additional writing by Sonja Hakala
Cover design by Cynthia McFarland
Cover and interior photographs by Nicholas Whitman
Text design and production by Cynthia McFarland, Susan Bernier, and Erin Lincourt
Line drawings by Brigita Fuhrmann
Indexed by Northwind Editorial Services

Storey Publishing books are available for special premium and promotional uses and for customized editions. For further information, please call the Custom Publishing Department at 1-800-793-9396.

Printed in Canada by Transcontinental Printing

10 9 8 7 6 5 4 3 2 1

LIBRARY OF CONGRESS CATALOGING-IN-PUBLICATION DATA

Mailboxes / edited by G.E. Novak.
        p.   cm.
    "A Storey Publishing Book."
    Includes index.
    ISBN 0-88266-970-2 (pbk. : alk. paper)
        1. Woodwork—Patterns. 2. Mailboxes. I. Novak, G.E. (Glenn E.)
TT185.M2 1997
684.1'8—dc21   97-23280
                                                                                    CIP

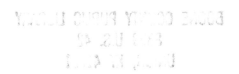

CONTENTS

Introduction to the Designs **4**

Part I: Mailboxes on Posts **33**

Bright-Eyed Cat **34**

Droopy-Eared Dog **37**

Funny Finny Fish **40**

Hummingbird **43**

Rugged Bunker Box **47**

Rustic Covered Bridge **50**

Log Cabin **55**

New England Barn **59**

House and Planter Mailbox **65**

Seaside Lighthouse **70**

Model A Ford **77**

Big Yellow School Bus **82**

Earth-Moving Bulldozer **86**

Autumn Sky **91**

Victorian Fruit Splendor **95**

Boxes for Every Season **99**

Part II: House-Mounted Boxes **101**

Oversized House-Mounted Box **102**

Herb-Lover's Garden **105**

Provençal Whimsey **108**

Privy Mailbox **110**

Mosaic Mélange **114**

Appendices **117**

Index **123**

Reading List **128**

Introduction to the Designs

WHO DOESN'T LOVE TO GET THE MAIL? Even in these days of faxes, e-mail, and the Internet, peering inside your mailbox and pulling out that slippery stack of catalogs, bills, magazines, and advertising circulars is still a pleasure, especially when it yields an actual handwritten letter or postcard, a birthday greeting, a party invitation, or your spring seed order.

BEGINNINGS OF RURAL FREE DELIVERY

THOUGH we take it for granted, delivery to a home mailbox hasn't been around for that long — just over 100 years, in fact. Rural mail delivery, free to the recipient, was first instituted as an experiment in West Virginia in 1896. Before then, mail delivery in this country was erratic and in rural areas, sometimes downright impossible.

Long before the letters RFD took on their current meaning, mail delivery had a long history. The most famous messengers of antiquity were the mounted express couriers of Xerxes, king of Persia in the 5th century B.C., employed to relay news about his invasion of Greece. The account of these celebrated postmen by the Greek historian Herodotus inspired the familiar words "Neither snow nor rain nor heat nor gloom of night stays these couriers from the swift completion of their appointed rounds."

The most famous name in early American postal history is Benjamin Franklin, who was appointed the first

◀ *Seaside Lighthouse, page 70*

Rustic ▶
Covered Bridge
page 50

Postmaster General under the Continental Congress in 1775. His reforms of the postal service included speeding up delivery times until it took only three weeks for a round trip of letter and reply between Philadelphia and Boston, ensuring wider circulation of newspapers by post, and making the postal system self-supporting.

It took 124 more years before carriers began to bring mail to roadside boxes in rural areas. This service became very popular with farmers for whom a trip to the nearest post office was a major undertaking. Daily newspapers, delivered by carriers on horses, bicycles, buggies, and carts, now connected country folk with the larger world with news about everything from world events to regional grain prices.

Log Cabin, page 55 ▶

Creating the Setting

A CUSTOMIZED MAILBOX is just part of the first impression you create for your home. Before you forge ahead on one of the projects in these pages, take some time to assess the spot you've chosen for your mailbox. Is it a candidate for a small bed of perennials such as phlox, lilies, ferns, or daisies? Could your mailbox be incorporated into a nearby fence? If you have wrought-iron lawn furniture, what about a wrought-iron post? Could the mailbox post serve two purposes and support an outdoor light as well?

Annual flowers can be part of the mailbox itself, like the House and Planter pictured below, or used to draw attention to a whimsical choice such as sunflowers around the Bulldozer on page 86, or sweet peas climbing the post supporting the Log Cabin on page 55.

Shrubs, such as lilac, forsythia, or juniper, and ornamental trees, such as crab apple or Japanese maple, can create an eye-catching backdrop. If your mailbox will be mounted on your house, consider repeating a favorite stencil or nature print on the spot just above your doorknob.

Remember, this is more than a mailbox. It's your personal greeting to every passerby. Express youself!

Planter boxes filled with vibrant flowers and foliage are wonderful complements to a handcrafted mailbox.

▲ *House and Planter Mailbox, page 65*

PERSONALIZING YOUR BOX

THE PROJECTS in the following pages are both beginnings and ends. You can warm up your jigsaw and create a colorful Barn that looks just like the one pictured below. Or you can paint it different colors, personalize it with your name, stencil the windows, or decorate it with found objects.

In other words, each of these mailbox projects is designed to get you started in the pursuit of your own creativity. In fact, there are suggestions for variations for each project at the end of each section. But don't stop there!

If you're a fan of flea markets and garage sales, keep your eye out for unusual metal buttons, wooden knobs, colorful ceramics, and light fixtures. When you walk in the woods, watch for

▲ *Big Yellow School Bus, page 82*

◄ *New England Barn, page 59*

▲ Earth-Moving Bulldozer, page 86

birch bark on the forest floor, unusual leaves, or a stand of willows growing near the edge of a swamp.

The next time you visit your local craft shop, lumber yard, architectural salvage yard, or hardware store, plan to spend a few extra minutes there looking for inspiration. While we suggest using herb stencils for the mailbox on page 10, you might be inspired by a new series of bird patterns to try your hand at a different motif. A decorative molding in your local hardware store may be just the right touch for the Barn mailbox you create. Or you might find a weathered door at your architectural salvage yard that would be perfect cut into strips for the Log Cabin on page 5.

Within these pages, you will find instructions for techniques as diverse as nature printing, stenciling, decorative stamping, and woodworking. Combine our expertise with your imagination to create a mailbox that is truly yours.

Model A Ford, page 77 ▶

▲ Mosaic Mélange, page 114

SELECTING MATERIALS

MAILBOXES, as well as mail carriers, must withstand snow, rain, heat, and gloom of night. In fact, your mailbox never has the chance to come in out of the cold and rain. Bear that in mind when it comes time to plan for your project. To paraphrase that old axiom, an ounce of planning is worth a pound of maintenance later on.

Wood Selection

Many of the wooden mailboxes, such as the Bunker box pictured at right, are constructed of plywood — exterior grade plywood, that is. For an in-depth discussion about materials, see pages 26–28. Even if you have pieces of scrap interior plywood around your shop, don't be tempted to use it for these projects. By the end of the first wet spring, the sides of your mailbox will be falling apart.

▲ Rugged Bunker Box, page 47

▲ *Herb-Lover's Garden, page 105*

▲ *Provençal Whimsey, page 108*

Paint and Finishes

When you select paints for any of the wooden mailboxes, be sure to use exterior grade latex or oil paints. And it wouldn't hurt to prime the wood before applying the paint. Priming makes a better bond between the paint and the wood, which means you won't have to repaint as often.

The creators of the painted mailboxes in these pages, like the Provençal Whimsey pictured above, use a wide variety of materials. Some of these colorants are appropriate for exterior use but some aren't. If your choice of paint bears the label "For interior use only," don't despair. Your artwork can be protected by two coats of clear spray varnish or polyurethane.

Grout and Ceramic

One of our mailboxes, the Mosaic Mélange on the previous page, is truly unique. The technique used to create this mailbox is called *pique assiette*, or bits and pieces.

The success of this project depends entirely on the ceramic pieces you find and the color grout you choose to use. Pick up colorful, chipped plates and mugs at garage sales or flea markets for pennies, add an odd salt shaker, the handle and spout from a cracked teapot, an old wooden spoon, a few ceramic whimsies, and a bright marble for your own unique version of the Mosaic Mélange. And choose your favorite color to add to the grout. The result is water resistant.

◄ Oversized House-Mounted Box, page 102

USING SURFACE DECORATION

MOST MAILBOXES come already painted, which makes them inviting blank canvases just waiting for your imagination.

Printing, Stenciling, and Stamping

If you're interested in crafts, nature printing is one you should consider adding to your repertoire. This simple technique (see Autumn Sky on page 15) works on the same principle as stamping but uses fresh leaves and printer's ink.

Stenciling, pictured in the Herb-Lover's Garden (page 10, top), is a traditional decorative technique using a pattern, paints, and a brush. Stencil patterns were originally made of thick paper, which made them susceptible to paint, but the new ones are created out of acrylic sheets. Stenciling is now so popular, there are new patterns in craft shops all the time.

Many craft, fabric, and interior design shops now carry sheets of flat, dehydrated sponge that are perfect for simple designs such as those on the Oversized House-Mounted box pictured above. Sponge stamps not only print on flat surfaces, they can shape themselves to any contour.

Privy Mailbox, page 110 ▶

Bright-Eyed Cat, page 34 ▶

SIMPLE ADDITIONS TO A STANDARD MAILBOX

WE BEGIN this book of mailbox projects with simple wooden patterns for the four animals you see here — the cat, dog, fish, and hummingbird.

If you've had limited experience with woodworking, these projects are a good place to start. They are cut from exterior grade plywood with a jigsaw, band saw, or scroll saw, sanded smooth, painted, and attached to the metal skin of a standard-size mailbox. If you start on a Saturday morning, your pattern pieces should be painted and ready to attach by Sunday afternoon.

In addition to creating the four creatures we've included in these pages, you can make your mailbox look like a favorite breed or pet. For example, if your grandmother dotes on a cocker spaniel instead of our Bassett Hound, enlarge a photograph of her pet and use it to make a pattern. This enlargement can be done photographically or via a color copier. Check around your local area to see which enlargement technique will best suit your needs.

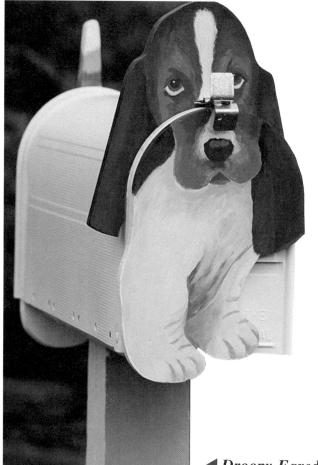

◀ *Droopy-Eared Dog, page 37*

▲ *Funny Finny Fish, page 40*

You can make patterns to replicate any animal with a head and tail for your mailbox. Why not try your hand at a rabbit, deer, horse, hawk, pink flamingo, or raccoon? Simply locate a picture of your desired critter in an information source such as a magazine or book. From there, follow the directions for making your own patterns that accompany the instructions for these four projects. To make sure it fits, cut your pattern out of foam board before cutting it out of plywood. And experiment with the painting details on paper first. A little planning will ensure your success.

These mailbox projects make great gifts because they are so adaptable.

◄ *Hummingbird,*
page 43

NATURE THEMES

EVEN IF your only seasons are hot and hotter, the natural changes around you can be reflected in your mailbox.

For example, the boxes on this page vividly express one artist's perspective on summer, fall, and winter while the stenciled box on the opposite page is yet another way to express a nature theme in your work.

Boxes for Every Season, page 99

▲*Victorian Fruit Splendor, page 95*

What are your favorite seasonal memories? Magnolias in bloom, clusters of juicy, red strawberries, cross-country skiing on a crisp January morning, or a breathtaking desert sunset are all subjects worthy of expression. Capture them in freehand designs like the boxes pictured on the page opposite. The artist who created them used brushes and cotton swabs for her designs.

Stamps cut from sponge open up all sorts of possibilities. What about stamping a starry night in June with a full moon or edging your mailbox with seashell shapes you remember from the beach?

Of all our mailbox projects, no other captures the natural world quite like Autumn Sky shown at right. The nature printing technique used to make this exquisite box is so adaptable you can replicate a sliced apple, a pressed pansy, maple leaves, and ferns on the same box.

▲ *Autumn Sky, page 91*

▲ *Shaker-Style Box*

THE ARTISAN'S BOX

OF ALL THE MAILBOXES we've seen, perhaps the ultimate synthesis of the classic, manufactured box and the personalized, handcrafted version is this Shaker-style mailbox. It was created by Harold Bigelow of Winchester, New Hampshire.

Though it is beyond the scope of this book in technique, this Shaker-style mailbox is not beyond the reach of the truly dedicated woodworker. Harold's box combines the strength and beauty of line expressed by the woodworkers who lived communally as members of the United Society of Believers in the Second Coming of Christ.

The Shakers, as they were commonly called, believed work was a form of worship, so their standards were high. During their peak in the mid-19th century, they produced tables, chairs, packaged garden seeds, herbal remedies, clothespins, barrels, cloaks, bedsteads, and their now-famous oval boxes for the "world's people," as they called non-Shakers.

They enjoyed a reputation for high standards of quality then and their simple, practical designs are revered now.

Harold recommends that anyone undertaking this project first master the technique of making Shaker oval boxes. Several good books exist on this subject. Check your local library or bookstore for information. Or, if you are fortunate enough to live near a Shaker museum, inquire about box-making classes.

Once you've mastered the technique, adapting it for a mailbox should be a relative cinch. Of course, you may not want to subject the finished product to the furies of the roadside and decide a porchside perch is preferable.

Have courage! It's not an undertaking for the faint of heart or short of patience. Harold begins his own process with trees from his own farm, which he selects and personally harvests.

It only goes to show — once you start hammering and tinkering in the workshop, you never know where it's going to lead.

POSTAL REQUIREMENTS

Most folks who have the urge to replace, fix up, or otherwise change their mailbox probably would not mention "aesthetics" if asked to explain what they're doing. More than likely they'd just say they want a better-looking mailbox. No matter how you say it, though, the U.S. Postal Service, like governmental agencies everywhere, has rules and regulations for the occasion. But don't be alarmed: The rules are simple and, unless you plan to go into business as a mailbox manufacturer, little trouble to comply with. In fact, postal regulations state:

Postmasters may approve curbside mailboxes constructed by customers who, for aesthetic or other reasons, do not want to use an approved manufactured box.

Most projects included in this book are built around, or are embellishments of, a manufactured, government-approved mailbox — so the postmaster will have no gripe, as long as you don't go totally overboard. Whether for manufactured or made-from-scratch boxes, the postal regulations are there to make delivery of the mail safe and convenient, and to protect the mail from the elements until you take it out of the box.

Other than actual placement of the mailbox alongside the road, which will be covered in the next section, the guidelines are fairly simple.

General Design Guidelines

► The mailbox should not be a safety hazard. That means no harmful projections, burrs, sharp edges, and so on.

► A curbside mailbox should be weathertight. That is, seams and joints should be tight enough to prevent loss or damage to mail.

Mailbox Markings

► Box numbers, if you have a number, should be at least one inch high and neat and clear, in a color that contrasts with the box itself.

When you add your name and house number to a mailbox, choose a color that stands out, such as red on white or orange on black.

► Your name may also be on the box.

► The markings should be on the side of the box that is visible to the carrier's regular approach.

► Advertising on the box or its supports is prohibited. (A newspaper tube may be attached to your mailbox post, but it should not touch the mailbox or obstruct the delivery of mail in any way.)

Door Regulations

► The mailbox door should open and close easily, stay securely shut when closed and not flop open, and not be spring-loaded. Magnetic latches are fine if they are strong enough to keep the door securely closed.

► You can put a second door on the back of the box, so you don't have to go out into the road to retrieve your mail, as long as it, too, stays securely shut and doesn't interfere with the roadside door.

Color Requirements

▶ Your box can be any color, as long as it is clearly visible in its surroundings. In other words, don't put a dark green box in front of a pine tree.

Flag Mounting

▶ The flag should be easy for the mail carrier to reach, and easy to see.

▶ It must be on the right side of the box as you face the box from the road. It should be no more than two inches from the front of the box when raised.

▶ The flag can be in any color that contrasts with the box except for any shade of green, brown, or white (trees, earth, and snow). The flag's color must not be used anywhere else on the box.

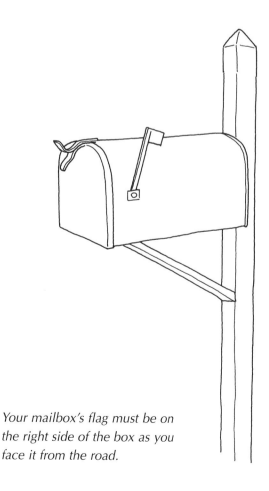

Your mailbox's flag must be on the right side of the box as you face it from the road.

PLACEMENT AND MOUNTING OF MAILBOX

The bottom of the box should be 3½ to 4' above the road surface, and the box should not project into the roadway itself. The main thing to keep in mind is the box should not be a safety hazard to motorists, yet should be easily reachable by your mail carrier.

You also want the box and its post to be sturdy enough to stay where you put them. That second part is not always as simple as it sounds, especially when snow plows are involved. But over the years homeowners have come up with many ingenious solutions, as any drive along a rural highway up north will attest. Some basic rules and suggestions follow.

Regulations for Posts

▶ Here's a direct quote from postal regulations: "Subject to state laws and regulations, curbside mailboxes must be placed to allow safe and convenient delivery by carriers without leaving their vehicles. They must be on the right-hand side of the road in the direction of travel by carriers on all new rural or highway contract routes . . ."

Although that might not tell you precisely how close to the road to put the box, common sense and simple observation will. See where other boxes are placed, and follow suit. Remember, the bottom of the box should be 3½ to 4' above the roadway. Ask the opinion of your mail carrier or postmaster if you're in doubt.

▶ Avoid overkill. The Postal Service advises against "massive mailbox supports that, when struck, could damage vehicles and cause injury." That includes concrete posts and old pieces of farm equipment, such as milk cans filled with concrete.

▶ Politeness counts. According to regulations, designs of posts must not include effigies or caricatures that disparage or ridicule any person.

▶ Some flexibility is allowed. Although the box should face the road, the arm attached to the box may be fixed or movable.

POSTS AND POST DESIGNS

Most of the projects in this book provide suggestions on how to attach a particular mailbox to its post. Those ideas, plus the following, can be adapted or modified to suit a particular design problem presented by a different type of post.

The Basics

An unadorned 2 x 4 post sharpened on one end and driven into the ground is the minimalist approach to mailbox support. Problem is, this setup won't last more than a few years, and may not be strong enough to hold a more substantial box. And it won't withstand even the lightest touch from a snowplow.

A step up, both in sightliness and durability, is a cedar fence post, especially if you prefer the rustic look. A pressure-treated 4 x 4 post is perhaps the most frequently used solution, and in most cases it is perfectly adequate for the job.

Most standard mailboxes are designed with a recessed bottom approximately ¾" deep. To attach one of these boxes, cut a piece of ¾" exterior plywood the same dimensions as the recess. Center and attach the plywood to the top of your post with three or four 1½" screws (sheetrock screws work well here). Slide the mailbox over the plywood. Attach the box to the plywood with screws inserted through holes in the side of the mailbox's lip. Voilà! You now have the basic mailbox attachment down pat.

Lap Joints for Post Arm

Step 1: Cut identical notches in vertical and horizontal pieces

notches cut out with chisel and hammer

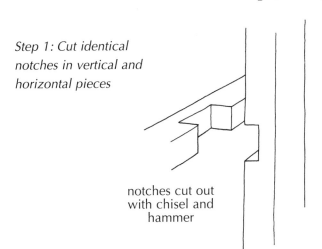

Step 2: Cross the arm and post at the notches and screw in place.

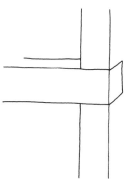

Alternate Version

Step 1: Cut notches as above.

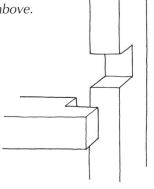

Step 2: Slip the horizontal in place against vertical and screw to attach. This is a weak joint and must be supported by a wood or metal brace.

Adding an Arm

The next step up in strength, if you're committed to wood, is a metal inverse L-shaped arm or bracket, available at hardware or home supply stores. Or drive around until you see a design that you like, make a mental note or even a sketch of it, and copy it in your workshop.

If you're using 4 x 4s, add a straight arm with a simple lap joint and support it with a metal or wooden brace. To make the arm illustrated below, lay the 4 x 4 you've cut for the arm across the post in the same position where the arm will be attached. Using a pencil, draw a line on both sides of the arm where it comes into contact with the post. Then draw a line on either side of the post where it comes into contact with the arm.

Using the saw of your choice (a table saw or circular saw would be best here), make several cuts close together between the lines on each piece of 4 x 4 at half the depth of the board. Using a hammer and chisel, dig out the cut wood until you have an identical notch on each board.

Cross the arm and post at the notches and attach the arm to the post with screws.

An alternate technique for the lap joint is similar except that the arm's notch will be cut in one end instead of somewhere along its length. Both of these arms must be supported by a brace.

Bracing the Arm

You can make your own brace of wood. Cut a piece of 4 x 4 pressure-treated lumber 18" long. Make a 45° angled cut on both ends of this piece so that the angles are made in opposite directions. (See illustration below left.) Attach this piece to both the post and the arm using four 1¼" wood or sheetrock screws.

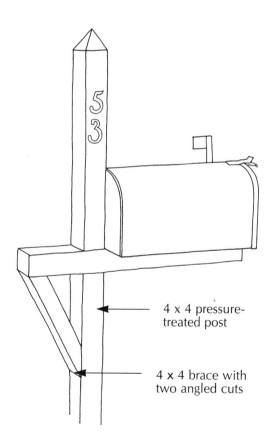

4 x 4 pressure-treated post

4 x 4 brace with two angled cuts

Given the sometimes trying conditions for roadside mailboxes, it's always a good idea to add a brace if your box is mounted on an arm.

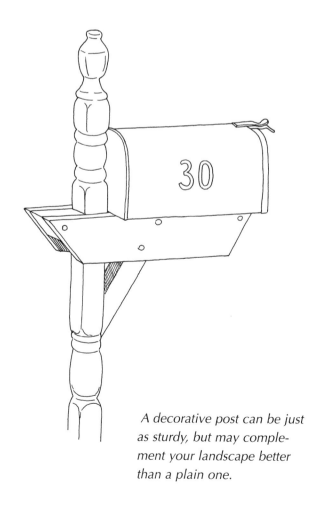

A decorative post can be just as sturdy, but may complement your landscape better than a plain one.

Still in search of inspiration for your mailbox post and attachment? For most home workshop enthusiasts, the only limits are cost and imagination — and any lack of the latter can easily be overcome by a drive in the country. This illustration features a large auger, used for digging post holes, as a whimsical post for a mailbox. Imitation, as they say, is the stepmother of invention.

A tapered top will help shed rain and snow, extending the life of the post. Your name or house number gets more attention on a metal hanger and plate above your mailbox.

If you choose to use a decorative post, such as the one illustrated left, your house number may be attached to the post itself instead of your mailbox. You can add another decorative touch by selecting a fancy metal brace to support the arm. In order to attach the mailbox to the arm, follow the instructions on page 19.

Mailbox posts do not necessarily need to be straight-sided 4 x 4s. There are lots of decorative posts available, such as the one illustrated on page 20. Add an arm to this post, following the instructions on page 20, brace it with a wooden arm described at left, then add two pieces of 1 x 6 pine to either side of the arm and brace, as illustrated. Paint or stain all the wood to match your residence or try your hand at a decorative technique such as stenciling (page 97) or nature printing (pages 92–94) on the pine.

Your mailbox will be attached to a mounting plate screwed to the arm as described on page 19.

Building Extra Support

Some of the mailboxes in this book will be quite heavy when you're done. For an extra-strong support system, cut two pieces of 2 x 4 pine, one 12" long and the other 20" long (see drawings below). Lay the 12" piece across the middle of the 20" piece at a right angle. Using a pencil, draw a line on both sides of the 12" board where it comes into contact with the 20" board. Flip the two boards over, keeping them in the same position, and draw a line on either side of the 20" board where it comes into contact with the 12" board.

Platform Support for Box

A

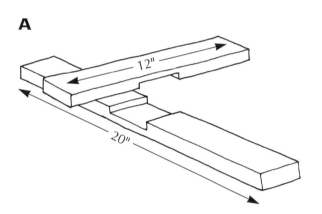

Once notches are cut in both boards, cross them to resemble the letter T.

B

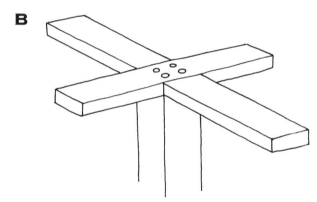

Once your post is in the ground, nail or screw the two crossed boards into the top.

C

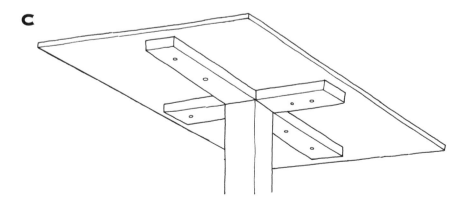

Cut a mounting plate from ¾ " exterior-grade plywood the same size as the bottom of your handcrafted mailbox. Working from the bottom up, screw the mounting plate to the crossed pieces of pine.

Using the saw of your choice, make several cuts close together between the lines on each piece of 2 x 4 at half the depth of the board. Using a hammer and chisel, dig out the cut wood until you have an identical notch on each board (illustration A).

Cross the 2 x 4s at the notches. Nail these crossed pieces into the top of your mail post (illustration B). Cut a mounting plate of ¾" exterior grade plywood big enough to accommodate your mailbox. Attach this board to your crossed 2 x 4s with screws, working from the bottom up (illustration C). Then attach your mailbox to the mounting plate.

Mounting Boxes with No Recess

If your purchased or handcrafted mailbox does not have a recessed bottom, you can attach it to your post by cutting two pieces of 2 x 4 the same width as your box. Attach these with screws to the front and back of your wooden post (see the illustration below left). Cut a mounting plate of ¾" exterior grade ply-

wood the same size as the bottom of your box. Attach the mounting plate to the 2 x 4s with screws, working from the top down. Lastly, fasten the mailbox to the plate with screws that are long enough to do the job, working from the bottom up. Be sure the tips of the screws do not come through the bottom of the mailbox. If they do, file their points flat with the inside of the box.

Going Metal

If digging a hole in the ground is not your cup of tea, or if the permanency of metal appeals to you, a heavy-duty pipe pounded in the ground with a sledgehammer has a lot to recommend it. If the pipe is threaded on at least one end, you can simply screw a floor flange to the top of the pipe (see illustration below). This can be attached directly to the mailbox with nuts and bolts or screwed into a piece of wood on the base of your mailbox. Just take care to protect any threads on the end of the pipe from damage. A

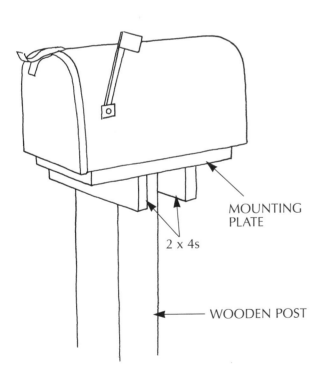

MOUNTING PLATE

2 x 4s

WOODEN POST

If your mailbox is older, it may not have a recessed bottom. This method of attachment will keep it securely on the top of the post.

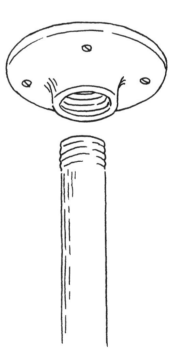

A pipe and floor flange arrangement makes a quick and sturdy support for your mailbox.

scrap of 2 x 4 to cushion the hammer blows will usually do the trick. The pipe can also be set in concrete (see page 26).

If snowbanks are a problem, you can start your pipe post farther in from the side of the road, then extend its reach to your mail carrier with a 90° elbow or two 45° elbows. These handy elbows, available at hardware stores and plumbing suppliers, make a trip to the welder unnecessary. Fasten your mailbox to the horizontal pipe with four L-shaped angle irons as in the illustration below. A tailpipe clamp, available at auto parts stores, is also handy to attach a box to a horizontal pipe system.

Remember, there's just about as much room for creativity in your mailbox post as with the mailbox itself. On the next page are just two design solutions that are particularly inventive — one completely utilitarian, the other to add a touch of greenery.

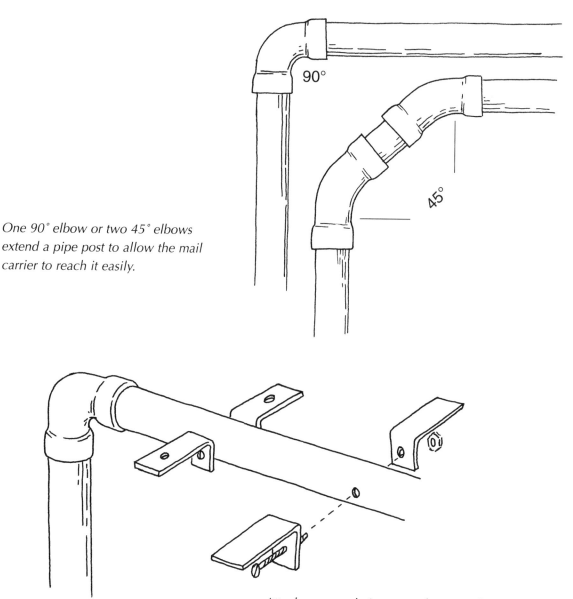

One 90° elbow or two 45° elbows extend a pipe post to allow the mail carrier to reach it easily.

Attach your angle irons to a horizontal pipe with nuts and bolts threaded through holes drilled through the pipe.

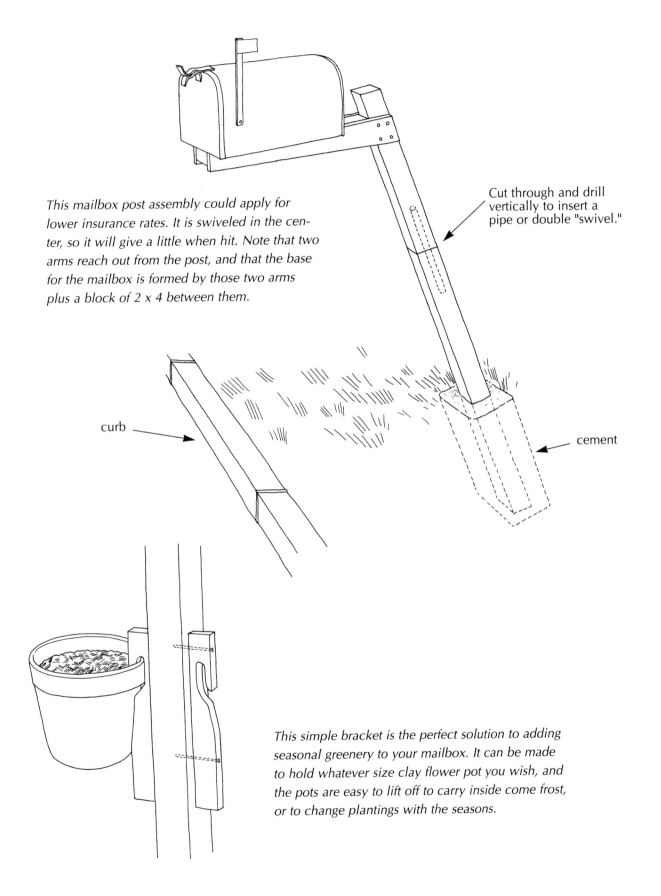

This mailbox post assembly could apply for lower insurance rates. It is swiveled in the center, so it will give a little when hit. Note that two arms reach out from the post, and that the base for the mailbox is formed by those two arms plus a block of 2 x 4 between them.

Cut through and drill vertically to insert a pipe or double "swivel."

curb

cement

This simple bracket is the perfect solution to adding seasonal greenery to your mailbox. It can be made to hold whatever size clay flower pot you wish, and the pots are easy to lift off to carry inside come frost, or to change plantings with the seasons.

POST INSTALLATION

If your soil is fairly rock-free, you may be able to simply pound in a metal post. If it's rocky, however, or you're using a wooden post, you'll likely have to dig. A post-hole digger will make the job much easier.

Generally, a hole two to three feet deep will be sufficient, although with heavier posts and boxes, two feet may not provide enough support unless you use concrete. The simplest method, shown in illustration A, is to dig a hole, set the post in the soil, then tamp earth around it. If the soil is sandy or unstable, a concrete base should be poured around the post, after it has been set in the hole (B). A temporary brace may be needed to hold the post while the concrete sets.

A

A post set in a hole 2 or 3 feet deep is strong enough for most mailboxes.

B

For more stability, pour a base of concrete in the hole, place the post in it, and fill the hole with tamped earth when the concrete is dry.

MATERIALS

Of all the potential problems you can face with a handcrafted mailbox, weather is by far the greatest. Your selection of materials and fasteners must always be made with this single factor in mind. Let's delve into this subject in greater depth so that you can make the best choices for your project, no matter which one you choose to construct.

Plywood

Plywood production probably saves more wood each year than a malfunctioning chain saw. It utilizes more of a tree than conventional milling techniques can, creates a very stable product, and if you're building a house, it covers more area at one time than pine 2 x 8s. Plywood is made of several thin sheets of wood, known as veneers, glued together in a panel, each veneer laid at right angles to the one before. This alternating wood grain means plywood expands and shrinks less than conventional lumber because each ply's action counteracts its neighbor's.

What does this stability mean for your mailbox? Well, it means the wooden sides of the New England Barn on page 59 won't warp as they withstand the rains of spring and the hot sun of summer. When you make your mailbox with exterior plywood, it will stay together a whole lot longer.

Plywood is made of both softwood and hardwood. Softwood plywood, which is made of trees such as Douglas fir, western hemlock, and ponderosa pine, is used mostly in construction where strength is more important than appearance. Hardwood plywood can be made of any number of hardwood trees such as maple, oak, cherry, or butternut. Much of the hardwood plywood in the U.S. is imported for use in cases where appearance is more important than strength, like wall paneling.

For mailbox purposes, your most important consideration is what type of glue was used in the plywood's manufacturing process. Exterior grade plywood is made with 100 percent waterproof glue so this is the only choice for a mailbox. Without it, your wooden mailbox would fall apart in a matter of weeks.

Lumber yards commonly carry 4 x 8 sheets of plywood in ¹⁄₁₆" to 3" thicknesses. Sometimes, if you don't need too much, you'll find half sheets. Unlike pine boards, a ¾" thick piece of plywood is really ¾" thick.

Sheets of plywood are graded according to the appearance of the veneers on the outside faces of the panel. Top quality faces are rated as N. The quality of others is rated on a scale of A to D, D being the lowest. Since all of the wooden mailboxes in this book are either painted or have a distinct outside and inside, you won't need to purchase the highest-grade plywood in the yard. For painted projects such as the Bright-Eyed Cat on page 34, find a medium-grade plywood such as B/C. For other projects, such as the Seaside Lighthouse on page 70 or the Rugged Bunker Box on page 47, you might want to choose a plywood rated A/C or A/D. These types of plywood are often referred to as "good-one-side."

Pine

Some of the wooden mailbox projects specify different thickness of pine as their building material. Be sure to check out the stock in your lumber yard thoroughly before purchasing it. Look at the end of the board. Is it flat across its width or is it cupped? Examine the length of the board. Is it straight from end to end or is it bowed or crooked? If it has knots, which are weak places in wood where a branch or limb was embedded in the tree, how many are there? Is there enough clear wood for you to make your project?

Be aware that a 2' x 8' x 1" pine board is not really one inch thick when you purchase it. It was one inch thick before it was milled. After processing, that board will actually be ¾" thick. A two-inch pine board is actually 1½" thick, and so on. When you're putting together your project, be aware of these differences.

Fasteners

The wooden mailbox projects in this book use a variety of nails and screws. Some designers specified the size and type of fasteners to be used, some did not. As always, common sense rules here. Brass

screws will not rust, so there won't be any discoloration bleeding through your carefully wrought paint job.

If you're attaching decorative pieces such as the chimney on the Log Cabin (page 55) or the willow branches on the Rustic Covered Bridge (page 50), nails are definitely the way to go. In fact, we've provided a nail chart on page 118 to help you make your fastening decisions. In most cases, finishing nails will be your best choice for these projects because their long, slender profile won't split wood.

Nails

Nails, along with waterproof glue, are fine for putting together the larger structural pieces of these projects together as well. But you could decide to screw them together instead.

Screws

Screws have more holding power than nails, and can be removed and replaced without damaging the wood. Of course, there are almost as many types of screws to choose from as there are nails.

First of all, screws are manufactured with three kinds of heads, round, flat, and oval. Unless you deliberately want to decorate your wooden mailbox project with exposed screw heads, choose flathead screws so that they will lie flush with the surface of the wood. Or, if you want a real nice finished look to your project, flathead screws can be countersunk, and their heads covered with wood filler.

A screw's size is expressed as two numbers, such as "No.8-1½"." The first number tells you the diameter of a screw's shank, the part you drive into the wood. The smallest number for commonly found screws is 0, which is .060" in diameter. The largest number is 20, which is .320" in diameter. The second part of a screw's size is the length of the shank. So a screw designated as "No.8-1½"" has a shank .164" in diameter and is 1½" long.

When you look at the shank of a wood screw, you'll notice it's smooth near the head, no threads. Choose fasteners that are long enough to allow the threaded, or bottom, portion of the screw to embed itself all the way into the second of the two pieces you are fastening together. For example, if you were screwing the back piece of the New England Barn (page 59) to one of its sides, the threaded part of the screw should pass all the way through the side piece then into the back.

If you're uncertain what fasteners to purchase, bring this book or a copy of the project into your local hardware store and ask for help.

TOOLS AND EQUIPMENT

With so many mailboxes to choose from, you're sure to find one that calls for all the craft or hobby tools you already have around the house. Or this just might be a great opportunity to try your hand at a new technique or to stretch your skills a bit. In any case, this equipment list covers all the tools you will find used in the following pages. But check the equipment list for each individual project before you begin to be sure you have everything readily at hand. We all know there's nothing more frustrating than discovering halfway through a project that you don't have all the right tools or materials.

Hand Tools

Clamps: There's nothing quite as handy as the extra pair of hands created by a pair of clamps. They hold wood in place while glue sets, keep a piece of trim in position while you drive in a finish nail, and can even help secure a stencil while you apply paint. If a project in this book requires a clamp, it's of the C variety, though pipe or wood clamps may be just fine for some applications.

Coping Saw: When you're cutting patterns out of wood, coping saws are a handy tool to have in tight places where a band or scroll saw might not reach. Coping saws can be used in place of a band or scroll saw for some applications.

Dremel: This handy little gadget, which is known by its manufacturer's name, functions as a small, hand-held drill, sander, buffer — you name it. This model maker's indispensable tool has lots of different bits and attachments and is available at your local craft shop.

Hammer: If you don't own one, now is the time. Not only will it be handy for making mailboxes, you'll be able to hang curtain rods, pictures, calendars, and crack walnuts.

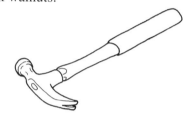

Handsaw: As with any cutting tool, be sure this is sharp before using it. More accidents are caused by dull tools than sharp. Many of the straight pieces for these mailboxes can be cut with a good, sharp handsaw.

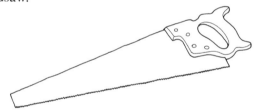

Measuring Tape: The best measuring tape to use for these projects is one of the metal types carried on the belt of every carpenter I've ever known. You can pull one of these tapes out six inches, lock it into place with a sliding button so you can measure twice (and cut once) then release the tape so it will slide back into place. A word of caution here — there is a metal catch tab at the end of these measuring tapes. If you let the tape snap back into its case repeatedly, the tab may break off and the tape retreat into its case never to be seen again.

Metal Snips: Like a hammer, a pair of metal snips can be invaluable to have around the house for all sorts of odd jobs. If you don't own a pair, you might consider indulging yourself in a good pair of snips. As with all cutting tools, be sure they're sharp.

Miter Box and Miter Box Saw: Not all the edges of these mailboxes sit at 90° from each other. Sometimes, they angle off and you'll need a miter box, equipped with the proper saw, to be sure all your angles are cut precisely the same. This process can also be done on a compound chop saw.

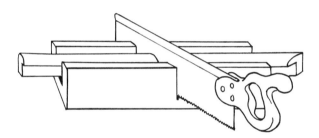

Nail Set: This tool resembles an oversized spike. When its tip is set on the head of a nail and its blunt end hit with a hammer, the nail will be driven lower than the surface of the wood.

Needle-Nose Pliers: The elongated jaws of this tool are perfect for holding small nails upright while you tap them in place or for twisting wire tight or any place else where a heavy pair of tweezers would do the trick.

Pruning Shears: One of our mailboxes requires gathering natural materials from the woods and pruning shears are just the tool for this job.

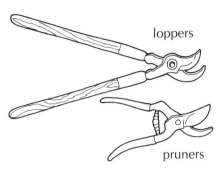

loppers

pruners

Ruler: Be sure the edge is free of divots and nicks. Metal rulers are the best because they keep a nice, straight edge.

Safety Goggles: Many carpenters, sculptors, metalsmiths, factory workers, and auto mechanics have blessed the safety goggles on their faces. You only have one pair of eyes. Why not protect them?

Scissors: It's always a good idea to have a pair of scissors designated for each material you intend to cut. For example, the pair you keep in the junk drawer may be used for all sorts of materials from plastic to metal. They would not be appropriate for cutting textiles or paper because the edge may no longer be smooth. Good, sharp scissors are not that expensive so indulge yourself in a pair just for your hobby or craft.

Screwdriver: There is a screwdriver for every occasion and every job. Screwdrivers come in flat or Phillips head, long and slender, short and stubby, small enough to tighten a screw in a pair of eyeglasses and large enough to attach a mailbox to a post. Check the directions for the individual mailbox to ascertain which screwdriver would best fit your choice.

Scraper: Great for spreading grout, removing old paint or wallpaper, or getting rid of extra glue, scrapers are one of those great, all-around tools to have in your kit.

Square: There's not much that's more frustrating than marking an angle on a board, cutting it, and then finding out that the angle is wrong. A good square is as valuable as a good measuring tape.

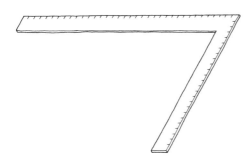

Tweezers: The small cousin to needle-nose pliers, these handy little items are indispensable.

Utility Knife: Better than scissors for cutting plastic or cardboard and they're always sharp, providing you replace the razor blades often. For an extra safety precaution, buy a utility knife with a retractable blade.

Wrenches: Like screwdrivers, there's a wrench for every job. Consult the directions for the mailbox of your choice to see if it requires a wrench and what type of wrench is needed.

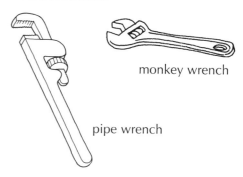

monkey wrench

pipe wrench

Power Tools

Some of the more difficult mailboxes require the use of power tools. Check the directions for the mailbox of your choice before starting on your project to be sure you have the tools required.

If you have never operated power tools before, please have someone with experience teach you the right way to use these powerful cutting implements before you set out to make a mailbox or any other woodworking project, for that matter. And be sure to wear your safety goggles.

Band Saw, Scroll Saw, or Jigsaw: Each of these saws features a thin blade and is designed to cut curves from wood. Thicker pieces of wood are best cut with a band or scroll saw. Jigsaws are often referred to as saber saws.

jigsaw

Chop Saw: The real name for a chop saw is a power miter saw. This power tool is best described as a small version of a radial arm saw because the cutting action happens from the top surface of the wood down. Unlike a radial arm saw, however, a chop saw's blade spins in an arm which is lowered to the wood. This tool is great for cutting wood on an angle and if you have a compound chop saw, you can cut bevels as well.

Circular Saw: This is the portable version of a table saw. If you're using a circular saw to cut your wooden pieces, be sure to have an appropriate cutting surface.

Drill: Electric drills probably rival jigsaws as the most common power tool found in a home shop. If you don't own an electric drill, check out the cordless, battery-operated variety before making a purchase. The lack of an electric tether makes a cordless drill even more useful.

There are a wide variety of bits available in your local hardware store. Be sure you have the right bit for the screws you plan to use before you start your project.

Radial arm saw: The blade in a radial arm saw whirls in an armature which is pulled towards the person using it. In addition to straight cuts, a radial arm saw can be used to cut on an angle.

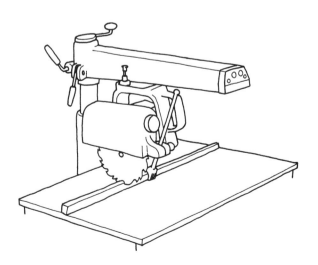

Sander: Probably everyone's least favorite chore, sanding moves along quicker if you have an electric sander. There are several types from small palm sanders that fit into your hand to large belt sanders that take up a lot of floor space in a shop. Be sure to read the directions for the mailbox of your choice to determine which type of sander is required for construction.

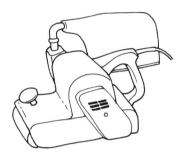

Table Saw: This cutting tool serves many functions, depending on what blade is mounted on it. This is an expensive piece of equipment that many people may not have in their shop. If the mailbox you choose to make calls for table saw, read the directions carefully. You might be able to go ahead with your project using a circular saw instead.

Other Special Equipment

Containers, Glass and Plastic: Some of the substances used in these mailboxes react badly to plastic so be sure to read the directions to determine what kind of container would suit your purpose best.

Low-Tack Masking Tape: Sometimes called drafting tape, this type of brown paper tape will lift from a surface when you want it to without leaving a sticky residue or pieces of itself behind. This is best found in an office supply or art store.

Paintbrushes: Cheap or expensive? Cheap or expensive? Paintbrushes come in all sizes and styles and bristle qualities. If you're going to use a brush just once and then throw it away, it might be worth purchasing a cheap brush. But be aware that less expensive paintbrushes have a tendency to lose their bristles easier.

Rubber Gloves: There are some substances, such as paint, glue, and grout, used in our mailboxes that are better kept off your hands.

Stencil Brushes: The process of stenciling requires a certain kind of brush. If the mailbox of your choice requires stenciling, read the directions carefully to determine the best one for your choice.

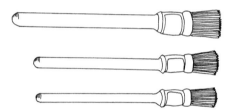

WHENEVER WE THINK of mailboxes, the style that comes immediately to mind is a standard-size, metal container with a rounded top sitting on a post by the side of the road. This sameness is, of course, a result of United States Postal Service regulations intended to make it easier for a letter carrier to deliver your packages, magazines, and birthday cards. However, while mailboxes are required to be of a certain dimension and height, and to be mounted so many feet from the road (see page 18), regulations allow wide latitude for imagination and creativity to be applied to the actual appearance of the box.

The first group of mailboxes you'll find in this section comprise a lively menagerie of easy-to-cut-out animal shapes. These colorful designs offer moderately skilled woodworkers the opportunity to create mailboxes customized to feature the pets and animals they love the most.

If you'd like to house your mail in a structure that complements your home and its setting, try one of the six miniature buildings that range in style from barn and log cabin to lighthouse, perfect for a seashore setting. One design even features "window boxes" in which to plant cheerful annuals and trailing vines.

The next set of designs you'll encounter takes its inspiration from the automotive field. These eyecatchers are a bit more complex than the patterns for the dog, cat, fish, and hummingbird, but if you have some woodworking experience and more sophisticated power tools, these vehicular mailboxes may be just right for you.

Finally, while some people love to work with wood, others prefer the silken glide of brush and paint. The last designs in this section offer instructions and lots of inspiration for one-of-a-kind mailboxes using a variety of painting techniques. Follow our patterns exactly, or use unique methods like nature printing and stenciling to forge ahead with a project that broadens your craft horizons.

Bright-Eyed Cat

MATERIALS

Government-approved, standard-size mailbox

¾" exterior-grade plywood

½" sheet metal screws

Acrylic paints

Water-resistant varnish or polyurethane

Spray adhesive (optional)

Sandpaper

EQUIPMENT & TOOLS

C-clamps (optional)

Drill (optional) with Phillips head bit or bit
    appropriate for the screws

Paintbrushes

Pencil

Screwdriver

Scroll saw or jigsaw

Please note that the materials list for this project
specifies ¾" plywood, which makes for nice,
substantial decorative pieces to add to a mailbox.
However, ¾" plywood is heavy and may stress the
sheet metal in a mailbox, so you should know that
this cat can be made with ½" plywood as well.

DESIGNED BY ALLYSON HAYES, SARATOGA SPRINGS, NY
PAINTED BY LISA HUNT, GREAT BARRINGTON, MA

Do YOU LOVE CATS, those purring objects of
poetry and Broadway musicals? Then this is the
mailbox for you. This simple design can be
painted to look like a Siamese, Burmese, or your
own favorite feline. To immortalize your
favorite cat, enlarge a photo and cut it into pattern-sized pieces for duplication. To be sure the
pieces fit your mailbox, glue the copy of your
enlarged photo on foam-core board, cut out the
pieces, and then shape them to fit the appropriate areas of your mailbox. Use these foam-core
pieces as patterns for cutting the plywood.

CUTTING

1. Enlarge the patterns illustrated on the opposite page for the head, whiskers, and tail using the
directions and grid provided on pages 120–121.

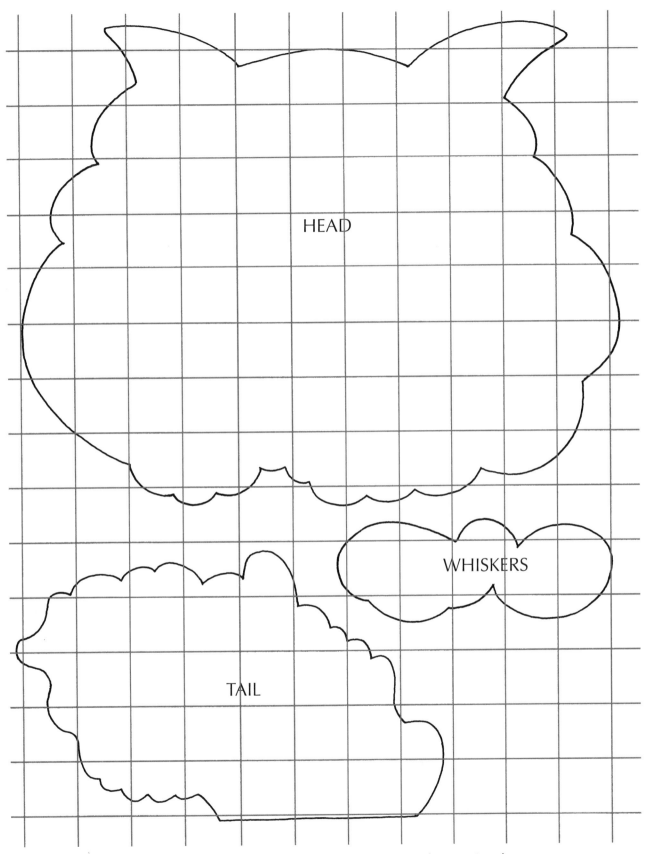

HEAD

WHISKERS

TAIL

One square equals one inch. Enlarge patterns above using the instructions and grid on pages 120–121 and trace onto plywood.

2. Trace the patterns onto the sheet of plywood, or attach the patterns to the plywood with spray adhesive.

3. Using a scroll saw or jigsaw, cut out each piece of plywood along the outside lines of the pattern. If you are using a jigsaw, clamp the plywood firmly to your work surface with the portion of the plywood you're cutting extending over the edge.

4. Sand the edges of the pieces until the saw marks are removed. This will help prevent splinters.

PAINTING

5. Using a pencil, sketch in the areas and dividing lines for the features on the face, feet, and tail. If desired, practice and plan your design by tracing each piece onto paper and painting the paper before starting on the wood.

6. Select a base color for the pieces (such as white) and paint the main areas this color, leaving the facial features open.

7. Use the other colors to add detail, building from dark to light with layers of color. Paint in the face. Add as many layers of paint as needed to get the desired effect.

FINISHING

8. Allow pieces to dry for at least 36 hours. Spray all sides with varnish or polyurethane to stand up to the outdoor elements.

9. Attach the pieces to the mailbox with ½" screws driven into the wood from the inside of the mailbox. An electric drill is handy to use in this process. Use two screws to attach the head, two for the nose and feet (these are attached from the inside of the door into the front piece), one for attaching the tail, and one each for the back feet.

FINISHING OPTIONS

MOUNTING
This mailbox should be mounted on a free-standing post without a back brace so the cat's feet and tail are visible. For mounting instructions, see page 18.

MAINTENANCE
Coat with varnish or polyurethane once a year to protect the wood from weather.

VARIATIONS
▶ If you're really inspired, paint the entire box to make the body of the cat match its adjoining parts.
▶ Get a cat breed book and enlarge a picture of your or a friend's favorite breed to make a pattern for a personalized cat mailbox for yourself or as a gift.

Droopy-Eared Dog

LEVEL: MODERATE

SEE COLOR PHOTO ON PAGE 12.

MATERIALS

Government-approved, standard-size mailbox

½" sheet metal screws

Acrylic paints

Water-resistant varnish or polyurethane

Spray adhesive (optional)

Sandpaper

EQUIPMENT & TOOLS

C-clamps (optional)

Drill (optional) with Phillips head bit or bit appropriate for the screws

Paintbrushes

Pencil

Screwdriver

Scroll saw or jigsaw

Please note that the materials list for this project specifies ¾" plywood, which makes for nice, substantial decorative pieces to add to a mailbox. However, ¾" plywood is heavy and may stress the sheet metal in a mailbox, so you should know that this dog can be made with ½" plywood as well.

DESIGNED BY ALLYSON HAYES, SARATOGA SPRINGS, NY
PAINTED BY LISA HUNT, GREAT BARRINGTON, MA

LET THE IMAGE OF YOUR FAVORITE DOG greet you at the driveway every day. This simple design can be altered to picture your favorite breed simply by enlarging a photo and cutting it into pattern pieces for duplication. To be sure your design fits the mailbox, glue the copy of your enlarged photo on foam-core board, cut out the pieces, and then shape them to fit the appropriate areas of your mailbox. Use these foam-core pieces as patterns to cut the plywood.

CUTTING

1. Enlarge the patterns illustrated on the opposite page for the head, front and back paws, and tail using the directions and grid provided on pages 120–121.

2. Trace the patterns onto the sheet of plywood, or attach the patterns to the plywood with spray adhesive.

3. Using a scroll saw or jigsaw, cut out each piece of plywood along the outside lines of the pattern. If you are using a jigsaw, clamp the plywood firmly to your work surface with the portion of the plywood you're cutting extending over the edge.

4. Sand the edges of the pieces until the saw marks are removed. This will help prevent splinters.

PAINTING

5. Using a pencil, sketch in the areas and dividing lines for the features on the face, feet, and tail. If desired, practice and plan your design first by tracing each piece onto paper and painting the paper before starting on the wood.

6. Select a base color for the pieces (such as white) and paint the main areas this color, leaving the facial features open.

7. Use the other colors to add detail, building from dark to light with layers of color. Paint in the face. Add as many layers of paint as needed to get the desired effect.

FINISHING

8. Allow pieces to dry for at least 36 hours. Spray all sides with varnish or polyurethane to stand up to the outdoor elements.

9. Attach the pieces to the mailbox with ½" screws driven into the wood from the inside of the mailbox. An electric drill is handy to use in this process. Use two screws to attach the head, two for the nose and feet (these are attached from the inside of the door into the front piece), one for attaching the tail, and one each for the back feet.

FINISHING OPTIONS

MOUNTING
This mailbox should be mounted on a free-standing post without a back brace so the dog's feet and tail are visible. For mounting instructions, see page 18.

MAINTENANCE
Coat with varnish or polyurethane once a year to protect the wood from weather.

VARIATIONS
▶ If you decide to make our Bassett Hound, add details such as large brown and black spots to the mailbox itself.
▶ Get a dog breed book and enlarge a picture of your or a friend's favorite breed to make a pattern for a personalized dog box for yourself or as a gift.

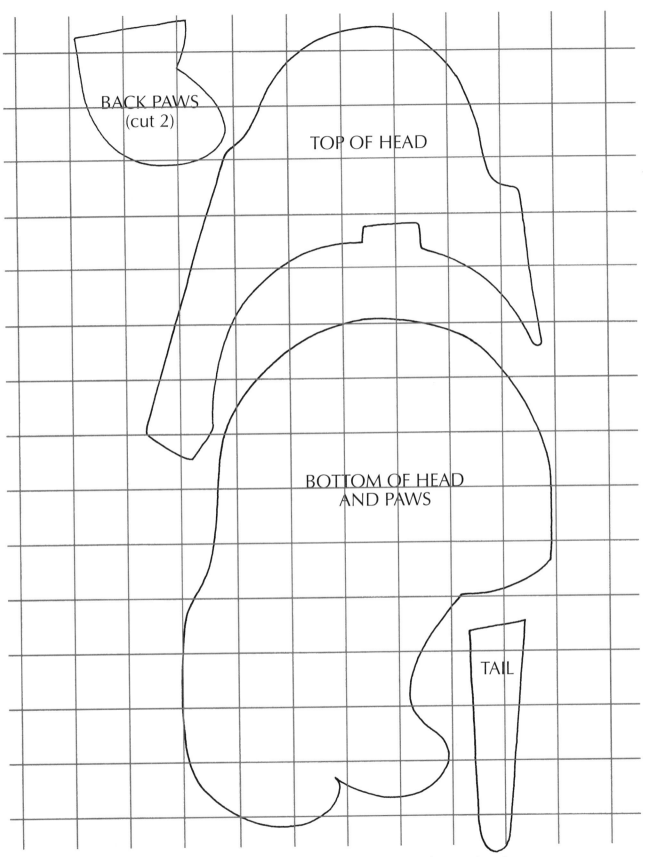

BACK PAWS
(cut 2)

TOP OF HEAD

BOTTOM OF HEAD
AND PAWS

TAIL

One square equals one inch. Enlarge patterns above using the
instructions and grid on pages 120–121 and trace onto plywood.

Funny Finny Fish

LEVEL: MODERATE

SEE COLOR PHOTO ON PAGE 13.

MATERIALS

Government-approved, standard-size mailbox

¾" exterior-grade plywood

½" sheet metal screws

Acrylic paints

Water-resistant varnish or polyurethane

Spray adhesive (optional)

Sandpaper

EQUIPMENT & TOOLS

C-clamps (optional)

Drill (optional) with Phillips head bit or bit appropriate for the screws

Paintbrushes

Pencil

Screwdriver

Scroll saw or jigsaw

Please note that the materials list for this project specifies ¾" plywood, which makes for nice, substantial decorative pieces to add to a mailbox. However, ¾" plywood is heavy and may stress the sheet metal in a mailbox, so you should know that this fish can be made with ½" plywood as well.

DESIGNED BY ALLYSON HAYES, SARATOGA SPRINGS, NY
PAINTED BY KATHERINE HUNT, GREAT BARRINGTON, MA

WHO NEEDS A TROPHY FISH when you've got this mailbox! It makes a great gift for fishing fanatics and river- or lakeside dwellers. The pieces of this mailbox can be painted to resemble a trout, perch, bass, or even a salmon. To immortalize your favorite catch-of-the-day, enlarge a photo from your preferred source of angling information and cut it into pattern-sized pieces for duplication. To be sure your design fits into place, glue the copy of your enlarged photo on foam-core board, cut out the pieces, and then shape them to fit the appropriate areas of your mailbox. Use the foam-core pieces as patterns for cutting the plywood.

CUTTING

1. Enlarge the patterns illustrated on the opposite page for the head, fins, and tail using the directions and grid on pages 120–121.

2. Trace the patterns onto the sheet of plywood, or attach the patterns to the plywood with spray adhesive.

3. Using a scroll saw or jigsaw, cut out each piece of plywood along the outside lines of the pattern. If you are using a jigsaw, clamp the plywood firmly to your work surface with the portion of the plywood you're cutting extending over the edge.

4. Sand the edges of the pieces until the saw marks are removed. This will help prevent splinters.

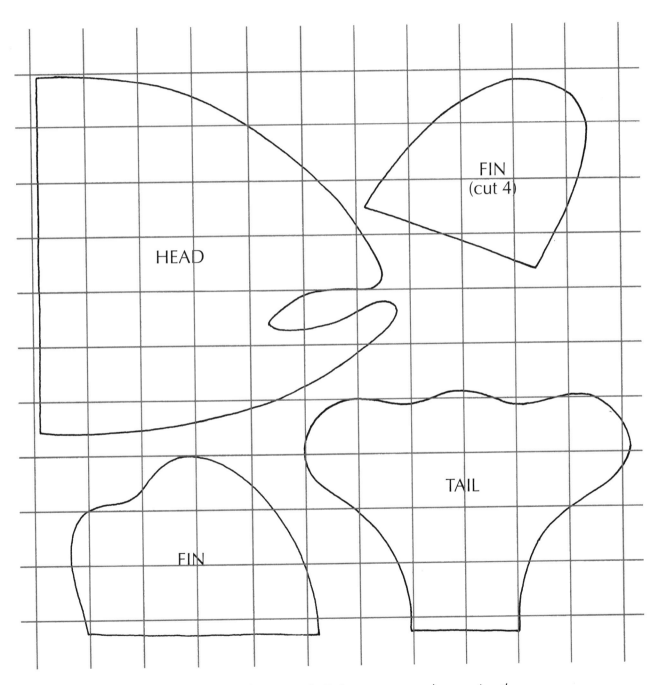

One square equals one inch. Enlarge patterns above using the directions and grid on pages 120–121 and trace onto plywood.

PAINTING

5. Using a pencil, sketch in the areas and dividing lines for the features on the face, fins, and tail. If desired, practice and plan your design first by tracing each piece onto paper and painting the paper before starting on the wood.

6. Select a base color for the pieces, such as pale green, and paint the main areas this color, leaving the facial features open.

7. Use the other colors to add detail, building from dark to light with layers of color. Paint in the face. Add as many layers of paint as needed to get the desired effect.

FINISHING

8. Allow pieces to dry for at least 36 hours. Spray all sides with varnish or polyurethane to stand up to the outdoor elements.

9. Attach the pieces to the mailbox with ½" screws, driven into the wood from the inside of the mailbox. An electric drill is handy to use in this process. Use two screws to attach the head, two for the tail, and one each for the fins.

FINISHING OPTIONS

MOUNTING
This mailbox should be mounted on a free-standing post without a back brace so the fish's tail is visible. For mounting instructions, see page 18.

MAINTENANCE
Coat with varnish or polyurethane once a year to protect the wood from weather.

VARIATION
If you're really inspired, paint the entire box to make the body of the fish match its adjoining parts.

Hummingbird

MATERIALS

Government-approved, standard-size white mailbox

Acrylic paints in appropriate hummingbird colors such as green, yellow, red, or blue with some black for details

Paper to transfer design

¾" exterior-grade plywood

10¾" screws

Water-resistant varnish or polyurethane

Spray adhesive (optional)

Sandpaper

EQUIPMENT & TOOLS

C-clamps (optional)

Drill (optional) with Phillips head bit or bit appropriate for the screws

Paintbrushes

Pencil

Screwdriver

Scroll saw or jigsaw

Please note that the materials list for this project specifies ¾" plywood, which makes for nice, substantial decorative pieces to add to a mailbox. However, ¾" plywood is heavy and may stress the sheet metal in a mailbox, so you should know that this hummingbird can be made with ½" plywood as well.

DESIGNED BY ALLYSON HAYES, SARATOGA SPRINGS, NY
PAINTED BY JULIA HUNT, GREAT BARRINGTON, MA

So MANY PEOPLE MISS THE CHANCE to see tiny hummingbirds as they whiz in and out of a garden. But no one will miss this gigantic replica when you add hummingbird details to your mailbox.

To make your yard truly hummingbird-friendly, surround your post with some of this bird's favorite flowers — morning glories, nasturtiums, columbine, phlox, and honeysuckle.

CUTTING

1. Enlarge the pattern pieces illustrated on the opposite page for the head, tail, wings, and wing support using the directions and grid on pages 120–121.

2. Trace around your paper patterns on the sheet of plywood, or adhere them to the plywood with spray adhesive.

3. Using a scroll saw, cut out each piece along the outside lines. This process can be done with a jigsaw but it is more difficult.

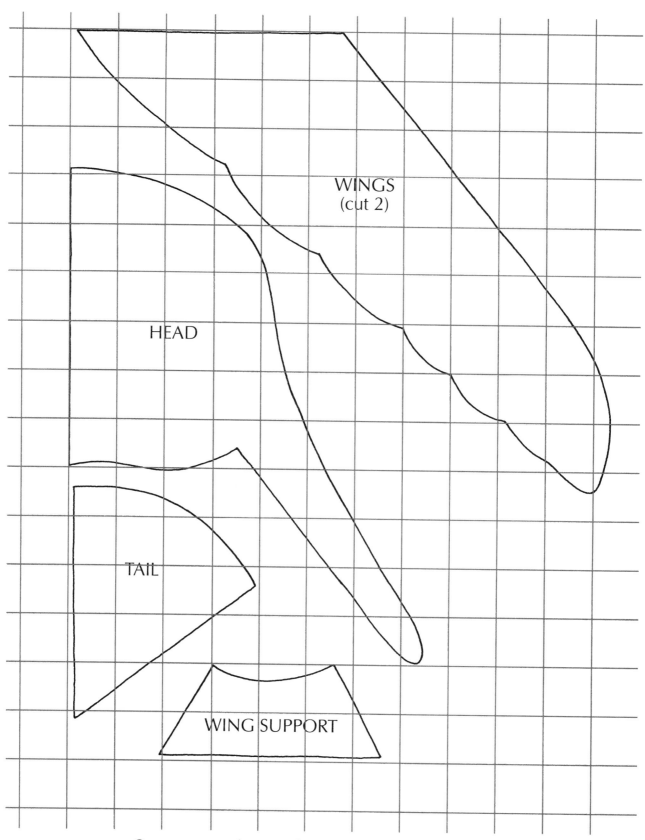

WINGS
(cut 2)

HEAD

TAIL

WING SUPPORT

*One square equals one inch. Enlarge patterns above using the
directions and grid on pages 120–121 and trace onto plywood.*

4. Sand the edges of each piece so the saw marks are eliminated. This helps prevent splinters.

PAINTING

5. Using a pencil, sketch in the lines for the eye, bill, and details on the tails and wing. If desired, practice and plan your design first by tracing each wooden piece onto paper and painting the paper before starting on the wood.

6. Select a base color for the pieces (such as green) and paint the main areas this color, leaving the eye and bill unpainted for now.

7. Use the other colors to add detail, building from dark to light with layers of color. Refer to the color photograph on page 13 for details.

8. Paint the eye and bill. Add as many layers of paint as needed to get the desired effect.

FINISHING

9. Allow pieces to dry for at least 36 hours. Spray all sides with water-resistant varnish or polyurethane to protect them from rain, snow, and gloom of night.

10. Attach the wings, using two screws for each wing, to the sides of the support piece.

11. Working from the inside of the mailbox, attach the head and tail pieces to the mailbox with ¾" screws, using two screws for each piece.

12. Attach the support piece and wings to the top of the mailbox, centering it, using two screws.

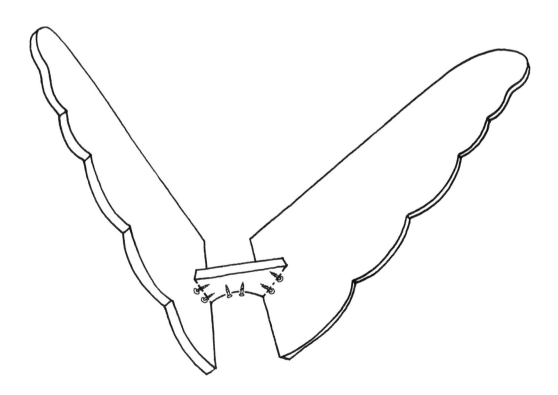

Attach support piece and wings to top of mailbox.

FINISHING OPTIONS

MOUNTING

Mount your mailbox on a free-standing post without a back brace so that the hummingbird's tail can hang off the back.

Follow the instructions on page 26 to put a mailbox post made of 4" x 4" x 6' pressure-treated lumber in the ground. Then attach the mailbox to plywood as directed on page 18.

MAINTENANCE

Reapply varnish or polyurethane to the wooden pieces of your hummingbird once a year to keep the colors true and to weatherproof the wood.

VARIATIONS

▶ If you're really inspired, paint the mailbox, which is now the body of the bird, so that it will match the hummingbird pieces you've added.

▶ Consult a bird guide to find out what species of hummingbird is native to your region and paint your box to match your native hummer.

Rugged Bunker Box

LEVEL: MODERATE TO DIFFICULT

SEE COLOR PHOTO ON PAGE 9.

MATERIALS

1 half-sheet (4' x 4') of ½" exterior-grade fir plywood, good-one-side, cut into:

   1 piece 8" x 12", back
   2 pieces 12" x 21½", outer sides
   2 pieces 11½" x 19", inner sides
   1 piece 9" x 21½", outer top
   1 piece 8" x 19", inner top
   1 piece 8" x 11½", door

1 piece, cut from 2" x 8" lumber, measuring 7" x 19", base

1 piece, cut from 1" x 2" lumber, 15" long, flag

1 piano hinge, ¾" x 6"

1 knob or handle

6 wood screws, #4, ½"

6 wood screws, #8, 2½"

1 lag bolt, 2"

Finishing nails, 1½"

Latex caulk

Sandpaper

Wood putty

EQUIPMENT & TOOLS

C-clamps (optional)

Hammer

Jigsaw or coping saw

Nail set

Stubby screwdriver

Table saw, circular saw, or hand saw

DESIGNED BY TOM CARPENTER, KINGSTON, ONTARIO
BUILT BY VINCENT RENE HART ROYCE,
NORTH BENNINGTON, VT

NOT ONLY IS this Bunker Box aesthetically pleasing, it will withstand assaults by baseball-wielding thrill-seekers and snowplows, a worthy consideration. It's made from half a sheet of ½" plywood and a 2' piece of 2" x 8" lumber, using basic tools and fasteners. That's it: cheap, plain, practical — and sturdy.

CUTTING AND ASSEMBLING

1. Cut all pieces to size as given in the materials list.

2. Apply an exterior-sealant latex caulk to the side edges of the base.

3. Attach the smaller side pieces to the base with 1½" finishing nails.

4. Caulk the top edges of the above side pieces and nail the smaller 8" x 19" top piece to them.

5. Apply a bead of caulk to the back edges of the top, sides, and base, then nail on the 8" x 12" back piece so that it lines up flush all the way around.

What you have at this point already looks much like a finished box, and with inside dimensions of 7" x 10" x 19", it more than meets the U.S. Postal Service's requirement for an inside size of 5" x 6" x 18½". You could attach a door and be done, but if you want a watertight, truly lout-proof bunker box, continue with the following steps.

6. You're going to be laminating the larger pieces on to their smaller counterparts. Each time you laminate one piece of plywood to another, you need to be sure the two bond tightly. You can snug them up with C-clamps if you have them. If not, take the time to drill a couple of holes in the smaller sides and top. Once you laminate the outer pieces to the smaller, use a stubby screwdriver to reach inside the box and draw the two pieces close together with ¾" wood screws.

7. Spread liberal amounts of caulk on one of the sides of the box, and lay one of the larger side pieces on it with the good side out. It should be even all around with the existing box except in extending 2" past the front. Make sure the two sides are bonded tightly, then nail the larger piece to the smaller along their top and bottom edges.

8. Repeat step 7 on the opposite side.

9. Spread caulk over the smaller top piece and lay the larger top piece on it. Make sure the two pieces are bonded tightly, then nail the larger top piece in place, lining it up in the same manner as the sides.

10. Turn the box on its side, and countersink three 2½" #8 wood screws through the side walls into the solid 2" base — one near the front, one near the back, and one in the middle. Flip the box over to install three more screws on the opposite side.

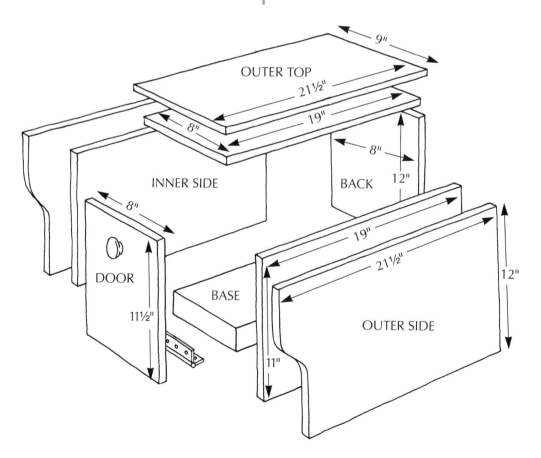

Exploded drawing shows how to assemble pieces.

11. Mount the door of the box using a 6" piano hinge, available at a hardware store. In the United States, the door must be hinged at the bottom. Using ½" wood screws, screw the hinge onto the inside surface of the door then to the bottom front of the base. Add a knob or other type of handle, then swing the door closed. If it's snug and stays closed by friction, good. If not, you'll need to add some type of cupboard clasp to keep it from flopping open.

12. For a decorative flourish, cut a pattern into the side pieces where they project at the front. Copy a simple curve, or try for something more whimsical. But leave the full overhang in place across the top and part way down the sides to help shield the door from the elements.

MOUNTING THE FLAG

13. For the flag, a simple 15" piece of 1" x 2" wood will do, painted any color but green, brown, white, or the same color as the mailbox itself (so that it stands out from grass, dirt, snow, and the side of the box). Use a 2" lag bolt to mount the flag into the thick base of the box about 2" from its front edge. Twist it in tightly so that the flag stays upright after it has been raised. Regulations require the flag to be on the right side of the mailbox when viewed from the front.

FINISHING

14. Sand everything, set all the visible nail heads, fill the holes, then coat the whole box, inside and out, with the best sealer-primer you have in your store of old paint. Apply a colorful finish coat (on the theory that the snowplow driver will see it) or perhaps basic black (in the hope that bat-wielding morons won't).

FINISHING OPTIONS

MOUNTING
Place the bunker box centrally on your post, and trace the post on the bottom of the box. Remove the box, and within the circle you've drawn, drill three ½" holes. Set the box back on the post, then tap the pointed end of ½" x 4" furniture bolts firmly into each hole from the inside of the box (furniture bolts are bolt-threaded on one end and screw-threaded on the other). Remove the box, leaving the bolts behind in the post. Tighten the bolts in the post by placing two nuts on the bolt end and twisting them with a wrench. Finally, set the box back in place, and secure it with a washer and nut on each threaded bolt.

MAINTENANCE
Check the box once a year to see if it needs a new coat of sealer.

VARIATIONS
▶ Paint your name and/or street number on the side of the box in a contrasting color.
▶ The outside of this box lends itself to lots of decorative techniques including stenciling (page 97), or stamping (pages 103–104).

Rustic Covered Bridge

MATERIALS

Government-approved, standard-size mailbox

6 pieces of ¾" pressure-treated plywood cut into:
   1 piece 7" x 19", bottom
   2 pieces 8¾" x 19¾", sides
   1 piece 7" x 14", back

1 piece 6¼" x 22", roof (A)

1 piece 7" x 22", roof (B)

2 pieces ⅜" plywood cut into:
   1 piece 7" x 17½", bottom insert
   1 piece 9¼" x 6⅝", to fit front door
   (optional, or you may paint the door or
   leave it blank)

Small block of wood, 2½" x 2" x 1½"

Bundle of freshly cut willow shoots approximately
   ⅜"–½" thick and 4' long. A bundle should be
   approximately 8" in diameter.

6 pieces of birch bark cut as follows:
   2 pieces 8" x 10" (one piece is optional)
   2 pieces 3" x 15½"

   (Note: Be sure to take bark only from a
   fallen tree in the forest or that you find on
   the forest floor. Taking bark from a living
   birch will harm the tree.)

5d galvanized box nails (approximately 35)

6 common nails, ¾" long

1 lb. box of 2d finish nails (1") **OR** box of
   18 gauge 1" pin nails if using electric pin nailer

4 galvanized flathead screws, #5 x 2"

1 flathead wood screw, #8 x 2"

4 oz. bottle wood glue

Pint of protective water sealer

DESIGNED BY DONALD MCAULAY,
STRICKLY STICKS, ERVING, MA

THERE ARE DOZENS of beautiful and sturdy covered bridges still in use all over northern New England and upstate New York. This project will give you a beautiful and sturdy mailbox.

EQUIPMENT & TOOLS

Anvil-type pruning shears

Circular saw or table saw

Electric drill with ¹⁄₁₆", ⅛", and ¼" bits and
   countersink

Electric pin nailer (optional)

Hammer

Saber saw or jigsaw

Scissors

Screwdriver

Tape measure

Utility knife

HOW TO IDENTIFY WILLOW

There are six common types of willows growing in the United States and Canada. All are characterized by long, flexible branches that sway in the breeze and slender leaves that are pointed on each end. They are most commonly found in wetland areas such as river banks and swamps. The six types of willow are:

▶ **Shining willow,** a hardy, tough tree indigenous to an area that stretches from Labrador to eastern Saskatchewan down to Iowa and over to New Jersey.

▶ **Coastal plain willow**, a bushy tree that is frequently found in the roadside ditches of coastal regions from Virginia to Texas.

▶ **Mackenzie willow,** which resembles the coastal plain willow but grows in the coastal regions from the Yukon to California.

▶ **Babylon willow,** originally from China. This graceful tree's shoots are pale yellow-green in the spring and olive-brown by winter. It is most commonly found in the area between Philadelphia, PA, and Washington, D.C., but specimens do grow as far south as the coastal plain of Texas.

▶ **Weeping willow,** which has bright yellow shoots in the spring, making it stand out against a dull background early in the season. During the summer, its foliage is a paler green than other hardwoods. It is quite common from southern Canada and the northern U.S. as far west as Minnesota.

▶ **Dragon's claw willow,** less common than the others listed above. Its foliage arrives early and stays late in the year. It is found in Canada from Ontario to Alberta and as far south as Indiana.

CUTTING

1. Cut all the ¾" plywood pieces to length.

2. Following the illustration, cut one long edge of the two side pieces and two roof pieces at a 30° angle. This cut is most easily done with a table saw but can be managed with a circular saw that has an adjustable table.

3. Cut all the ⅜" plywood pieces to length. If you decide to use this plywood for the optional front door cover, trace the outline of the metal mailbox's door on the 9¼" x 6⅝" piece of plywood and cut the curve with a saber saw or jigsaw.

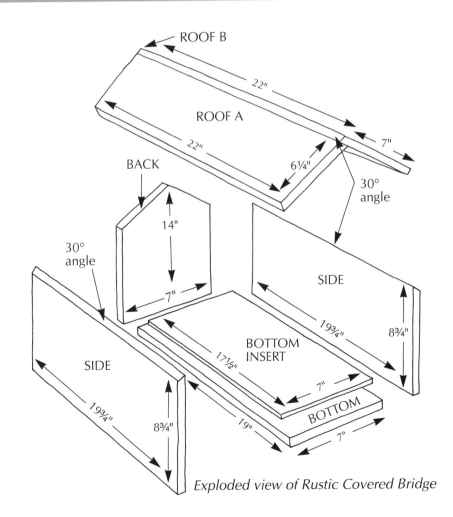

Exploded view of Rustic Covered Bridge

4. Measure up from the bottom (one of the 7" sides) of the back piece 8¾ ". Mark this spot. Find the center point of the top edge of the back. Mark this spot. Draw a line connecting these two points and draw a line. Cut off this small triangle of wood. Repeat this step for the other side. When you are done, the top of the back piece will be cut to make the peak of the roof of the bridge.

5. Using a utility knife or scissors, cut the two 8" x 10" birch bark pieces as illustrated below.

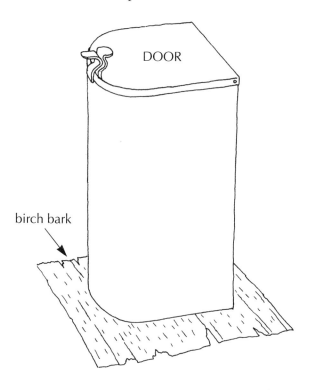

birch bark

ASSEMBLING

6. Nail the ⅜" insert piece onto the top of the bottom piece using ¾" nails. The two pieces should be flush on both sides and the rear.

7. Nail the back piece to the bottom piece, making sure they are flush with one another, using 5d galvanized nails.

8. Nail both side pieces to the back and bottom using 5d galvanized nails.

9. Nail roof piece (A) to the back and one of the side pieces with 5d galvanized nails. The 30° angle of the roof piece should be flush with the peak of the back piece, allowing the roof piece to overhang the side piece by 1". Helpful hint: To find the correct nailing position, measure 2" up from the bottom of the roof piece and draw a line across the topside of the wood. Nail along this line.

10. Nail roof piece (B) to the back, one side, and roof piece (A) with 5d galvanized nails, making certain the 30° angle is flush at the peak of the back piece, and allowing a 1" overhang over the side.

11. Locate two points on the back piece, measuring up 1⅝" from the bottom and 2" in from both sides. Drill two holes in these locations using a ⅛" drill bit and countersink.

12. Locate one point on each of the two sides by measuring up 1⅝" from bottom of both sides and 4½" in from the front opening. Drill one hole on each side with ⅛" drill bit and then countersink the holes.

13. If you want to use the optional plywood front door, first remove the latch mechanism from the metal mailbox. Use the nuts and bolts from the latch to attach the plywood front door to the metal door. The latch should be between the plywood and the door of the metal mailbox. Glue birch bark to the plywood using wood glue. Outline the bark with willow shoot using 2d finish nails.

14. Insert the metal mailbox into the front opening of your covered bridge. Secure it by firmly pushing the mailbox down and toward the back.

15. Using a ¹⁄₁₆" drill bit, drill through existing ⅛" holes in the back and sides of the bridge box (see step 12). Insert 2" x ⅛" galvanized screws into all holes and, using a screwdriver, secure the mailbox within.

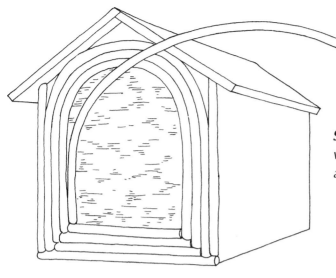

Step 17: *Outline the false back with willow shoots, bending slowly to create an arch.*

Steps 18–21: *Use small pieces of willow to decorate the interior of the bridge's windows. Nail pieces of willow to the roof's peak and both roof lines to act as guides for covering the remainder of the roof.*

FINISHING THE ROOF, DOOR, AND WINDOWS

16. Glue the second birch bark door piece ¾" up from the bottom edge of the back piece to create a covered bridge opening.

17. Outline this false birch bark door with freshly cut willow shoots, bending them slowly to create an arch. Nail and secure.

18. Turn the mailbox onto one side. Glue one 3" x 15½" piece of birch bark 3½" up from bottom and 2½" in from the back. This will be one of the bridge's windows. Repeat on the other side.

19. Outline the birch bark with willow shoots and inlay Xs to complete the window effect.

20. Outline the front of the mailbox by nailing willow to the outside edges of the side pieces using 2d finish nails.

21. Nail a piece of willow to the peak of the roof to act as a guide as you cover the rest of the roof with willow shoots. Nail a piece of willow along both roof lines to act as a guide also. Starting at the peak, cover both sides of the roof with willow shoots using 2d finish nails. Box in the ends with slightly smaller willow shoots.

MOUNTING THE FLAG

22. Remove the flag from the metal mailbox. Position the 2½" x 2" x 1½" wooden block on the right side of the covered bridge 5" up from the bottom and ½" back from the front. Attach the block to the box by drilling a hole in the block and screwing it to the covered bridge with one #8 x 2" flat-head wood screw. Use the existing mailbox hardware to attach the flag and flag assembly to the block.

FINISHING THE SIDES AND BACK

23. Cover the sides of the box with willow shoots, using 2d finish nails. Try to use willow shoots of similar size on the sides, back, and roof. Use smaller willow shoots to trim the roof ends.

24. Cover the back of the box with willow shoots, bending them to follow the outline of the estalished arch using 2d finish nails.

FINISHING OPTIONS

MOUNTING
Follow the instructions on page 26 to put a mailbox post made of 4" x 4" x 6' pressure-treated lumber into the ground. Cut a piece of ¾" pressure-treated plywood the same size as the bottom of your covered bridge. Attach it to the top of your post with 1¼" wood screws, letting approximately two-thirds of the plywood overhang the post on its street side.

Cut a piece of 4" x 4" x 6' pressure-treated lumber 18" long. Make a 45° angled cut on both ends of this piece so that the angles are made in opposite directions. (See diagram on page 22.) Attach this piece to both the post and the plywood using four 1¼" wood screws.

Put your covered bridge mailbox on the plywood so that the front and back of the mailbox are flush with the front and back of the plywood. Working from the bottom up, attach the mailbox to the plywood with four 1¼" wood screws. If the points of the screws protrude into the box, file them flush with the interior of the mailbox.

MAINTENANCE
Coat the covered bridge with wood sealer once a year.

VARIATIONS
▶ The front door can be birch bark or plain white.
▶ Paint your name on the door of the mailbox or fasten a nameplate to it.
▶ Attach a nameplate to the ridge of the roof.
▶ An address or numberplate may be attached below the window on the right side.

Log Cabin

LEVEL: MODERATE TO DIFFICULT
SEE COLOR PHOTO ON PAGE 5.

MATERIALS

Government-approved, standard-size black mailbox

2 pieces 1" x 12" x 8' pine (the rougher and more weathered the better)

Rip one 8' piece into strips ¾" wide and cut them as follows:

    5 pieces 7¼" long
   10 pieces 22" long
    8 pieces 15¾" long
    8 pieces 2½" long
    4 pieces 12" long
   14 pieces 10¾" long

From the second 8' piece, cut the following:
    1 piece 6" x 17½", baseboard for under mailbox
    1 piece 9¼" x 17¾", floorboard
    1 piece 10¼" x 22", roof
    1 piece 11¼" x 22", roof

White cedar shingles (about 20)

Copper flashing (optional)

2" screws, about 6

1½" screws, about 6

4d galvanized finish nails

6d galvanized finish nails

Exterior paintable caulk

1" galvanized small nails

½" galvanized small nails

Linseed oil, exterior stain, or exterior latex paint

Weatherproof glue

DESIGNED BY KATHE MOTTOR, EASTHAMPTON, MA

THIS MAILBOX WAS THE CULMINATION of a series of rustic birdhouses, which expanded to include this log cabin. Its design will give the illusion of logs overlapping at the corners without going through the process of notching them to fit.

The log cabin is of moderate difficulty to construct. Being comfortable with saws and imagination should prove helpful.

EQUIPMENT AND TOOLS

C-clamps, optional

Drill, preferably battery-operated

Hammer

Jigsaw and/or chop saw or scroll saw

Measuring tape

Metal snips

Speed square

Table saw

ASSEMBLING THE CABIN

1. Begin laying out the walls of the log cabin (see illustration). Glue and nail the 22" strips, rough-side-out, flush with the edges of the floorboard. There should be about a 2" overhang at each end. The 7¼" strip should fit flush against the end of the floorboard between the two sides.

2. Glue and nail the second tier of "logs" over the first (see illustration). The 12" strip goes on the back end, flush with the outside, leaving a 2" overhang at each end. The 15¾" pieces are used for the sides, and the 2½" pieces are used for the front, with their overhang matching that in back. As the front pieces are attached, be sure to keep the inside edges of the wooden strips even with each other as they frame the open doorway.

3. Repeat Steps 1 and 2 until you've used all the pieces of those sizes. Use about 4 finish nails (4d) per strip and exterior weatherproof glue to attach the strips to one another.

ATTACHING THE ROOF AND CUTTING THE GABLES

4. The roof of this log cabin is a gable, which means it slopes down in two directions from the center line of the cabin. To make the gable (angled) ends, take seven of the 10¾" strips and stack them (see illustration at right). Using a speed square, draw two 45° angles on the stacked strips and then cut them using your chop saw. If you don't have a speed square, simply place a mark at the top center of the stack and draw lines from it to each of the bottom corners. Clamp the strips together using a C-clamp and cut them using a jigsaw.

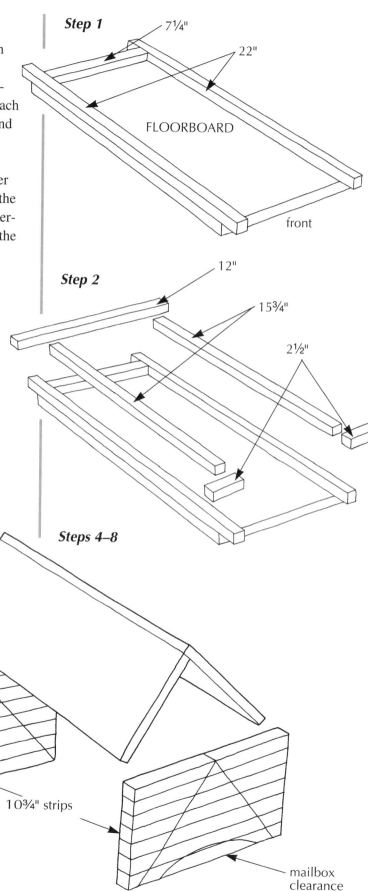

Step 1

7¼"

22"

FLOORBOARD

front

Step 2

12"

15¾"

2½"

Steps 4–8

10¾" strips

mailbox clearance

5. Working up from the top of the back wall, glue and nail each piece of the back gable in place, working from largest to smallest until the triangle is complete.

6. Stack the remaining seven 10¾" strips against the completed gable on the inside of the log cabin. Trace the outline of the first gable onto the stacked boards to get your second triangle. Slip the mailbox into the box and trace the outline of the box onto the second gable. The mailbox's outline will give you the clearance you need to re-insert the box once you've completed the log cabin.

7. Remove this second stack of gable pieces and cut out the triangle and clearance for the mailbox.

8. The roof is a simple overlap (see illustration). Line up the 10¾" x 22" board flush with the points of the two gables. Glue and nail (with 6d nails) this roof piece to the gable ends.

9. Take the remaining roof section, glue and nail it to the first roof section and the gable ends, keeping it flush with the top of the first board.

10. Take a couple of pieces of scrap or cut new pieces of pine to trim the ends of the gables before attaching the white cedar shingles to the roof.

SHINGLING THE ROOF

11. Lay out the cedar shingles on the roof. This first layer of shingles should be cut so that their top edges fit flush with the peak of the roof, overhang the bottom edge of the roof by at least an inch, and overhang the gable ends of the roof by ⅛" (see illustration below). Glue, then nail these shingles in place using the 1" nails along the top of each shingle and one-third of the way down from the top along each side of the shingle. These nails will be covered by a second row of shingles.

12. The second row of shingles should be approximately half the length of the first row. When you lay this second shingle layer down, be sure you overlap the joint below by at least 1". Nail these shingles along the top edge with 1" nails plus one nail near the bottom in each corner.

13. There are three ways to cover the peak.

▶ Nail a 2" wide strip of copper flashing with copper nails along the peak.
▶ Glue and then nail two strips of ½" thick wood — one of them 1½" wide and the other 2½" wide — so that they overlap at the peak.
▶ Cut a 2" strip from a coffee can to cover the peak and nail it in place.

DECORATING

14. The basic structure is complete. You can now decorate with windows and doors, add a chimney, or leave it plain. To make a chimney, cut a piece of scrap to your desired width, place it against a gable end and trace the roof angle onto the scrap. Cut the angle, then nail the chimney about midway on the roof and caulk it in place. Paintable caulk works best.

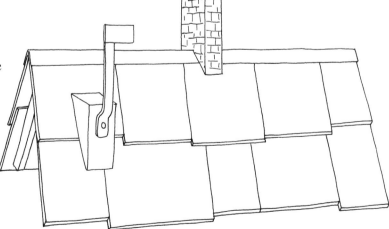

Steps 11–13: Your first layer of shingles should stretch from the peak of the roof to overhang the sides by 1 inch. This illustration shows an alternative location for the flag mount.

ATTACHING THE FLAG

15. Remove the flag and its holder from the metal mailbox. The flag can be attached to the log cabin in several ways. Remember, U.S. postal regulations require a flag to be on the right side of the mailbox as it is viewed from the road. Please note, mailboxes come with different kinds of flag mounts so you may need to adjust the following designs accordingly.

▶ Using scrap, cut a mounting block for the side of the cabin. It should be wide enough for the flag to clear the eaves so that it will go up and down freely. Use the flag holder to determine how wide and tall you will need to make the mounting block. I used a piece of scrap cedar and chose to cover the block with leftover pieces of log to give a more finished look.

▶ Make a block from scrap (see illustration on page 57). Place the block along the gable edge of the roof, holding it vertical to the roof line, and draw your bottom angle so that the block will sit squarely on the roof when you attach your flag. Glue and nail in a position not more than 2" from the front on a solid part of the roof (not the overhang), and screw the flag on.

FINISHING

16. Prepare your log cabin mailbox for painting by filling gaps between the logs with caulk and sanding the surface smooth where needed. Let everything dry thoroughly before painting or staining. The mailbox on page 5 was finished with linseed oil on the cedar shingles, a brown oil-based stain on the logs, and exterior latex paint on the windows and doors.

FINISHING OPTIONS

MOUNTING
With boxes this large and heavy, it is best to use a 4" x 4" post with a flat-arm base with no back section to interfere with positioning the box.

▶ Attach the baseboard to the metal mailbox. Slide the mailbox all the way into the log cabin and screw through the bottom of the log cabin into the baseboard to secure the mailbox. Attach the whole unit to your wooden mailbox post by using four angle brackets to hold the mailbox in place.

▶ Cut a piece of exterior plywood or board slightly smaller than the floor of the log cabin. Attach this board to the top of your wooden mailbox post by screwing it in place.

Attach the baseboard to the metal mailbox. Slide the mailbox all the way into the log cabin and screw through the bottom of the log cabin into the baseboard to secure the mailbox. Position the whole unit on the board you've attached to the mailbox post. Secure your log cabin mailbox in place by screwing through the board into the floor of the cabin.

MAINTENANCE
Pine will shrink so cracks may develop between the logs of your log cabin. These can be filled with paintable exterior caulk then touched up with paint. If you see the wood is drying out, it's time to refinish.

VARIATIONS
▶ Instead of staining the exterior of the log cabin, paint it with exterior latex paint.

▶ Instead of covering the roof with cedar shingles, you can cover the roof with a sheet of 16-oz. copper flashing.

New England Barn

MATERIALS

One sheet ½" plywood, exterior grade, cut into:
   2 pieces, 11¾" x 19", sides
   2 pieces, 11¾" x 17½", front and back
   2 pieces, 9" x 20", roof
   1 piece, 11¾" x 19¾", base

7' of ¾" x 2½" lath strips, cut into:
   2 pieces, 18" each, for base
   4 pieces, 11" each, for sides
   1 piece, 8", for front

17' of ½" x 1¼" trim

4' of ⅜" x ¾" parting bead

2' of ¾" scotia (cove) molding

2' of 20" copper flashing (16 oz.)

¾" nails

Magnetic catch

One pair of hinges 1" to 1½" wide. (Be sure the hinges come with screws.)

Wood glue

Red acrylic paint and other colors such as blue or yellow (Refer to the color photograph of this project on page 7 for color ideas.)

Wooden drawer pull

3' of 2" x 4" pine (optional, for mounting)

Four 2" screws (optional, for mounting)

Two 4" nails (optional, for mounting)

DESIGNED BY CARL PHELPS,
GREENBRIER FARM, WILLIAMSTOWN, MA

ONE OF THE ADVANTAGES of this barn mailbox is that it doesn't require a government-size metal box for an insert. Its design was inspired by the many New England barns in the vicinity of Carl Phelps's Greenbrier Farm.

EQUIPMENT & TOOLS

Chisel (optional, for mounting)

Circular saw or table saw

File (optional, for mounting)

Hammer

Miter box and saw or chop saw

Paint brushes

Screwdriver (Check the screws that come with the hinges to determine the type of screwdriver needed.)

Tin snips

CUTTING

Much of the cutting in this project was done on a table saw, but if you feel comfortable and have an appropriate cutting surface, use a circular saw instead.

1. Measure and cut the plywood pieces for the two sides, back, front, roof, and base.

2. This barn has a gable roof, which means it slopes down in two directions from the center line of the roof. In order to form this roof, you need to make two angled cuts on both the front and back pieces. When you're done, these pieces should be identical and will look like squares with a triangle on top. Check the illustration below to get the correct measurements for this process. Now cut the gables — the angles — on your front and back pieces.

3. Cut a door in the front piece measuring 9" x 6¾". Be sure to cut up from the bottom 9" and over 6¾". Save the piece you cut out. This will eventually be attached by a hinge to serve as the door of your mailbox.

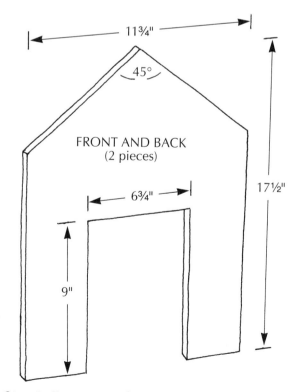

Step 3: Door cut in front only (save door cutout to make door).

ASSEMBLING

4. Cut the lath strips as indicated in the materials list. Glue and then nail them to the base, sides, and front pieces of the barn. (See top illustration on opposite page.) Always apply glue to the smaller of the two surfaces you are adhering. The lath strips will reinforce the structure and provide nailing surfaces. (Throughout this project, always glue as well as nail for extra strength.) The two strips on the base must be set in ½" from the edge. The strip on the front should be even with the top of the cutout for the door.

5. Mount the magnetic side of the catch to the underside of the lath strip at the top of the door opening. The outside surface of the catch should be flush with the inside wall of the plywood. (See bottom illustration on opposite page.)

6. Glue and then nail the sides to the front, making sure that the outer surfaces of the sides are flush with the outside edge of the front piece. In other words, the seam lines you create when you put the sides and front together should be visible from the side only. When you look at your mailbox from the front, you should not be able to see any seam lines. As you drive nails through the front and into the side pieces, be sure to drive one into the lath strips as well.

7. Once the front and side pieces are together, attach the back to the sides in the same manner as you attached the front to the sides.

8. Glue and then nail the wall assembly onto the base. You now have a roofless barn with a cutout door.

PAINT AND TRIM

9. Paint the barn with your main color choice.

Step 4: *Attaching the lath strips*

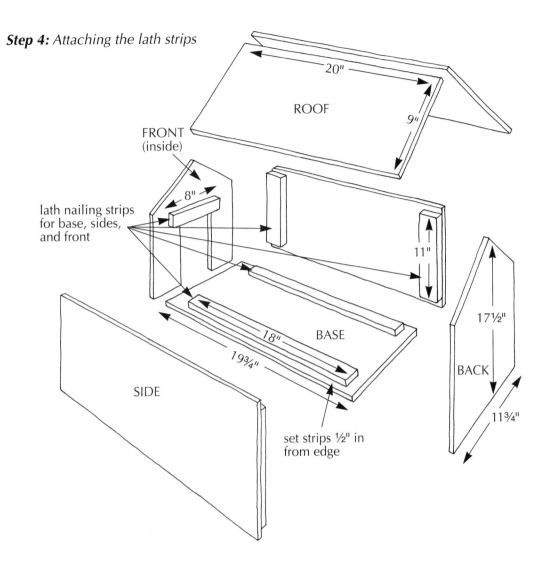

ROOF

20"

9"

FRONT
(inside)

8"

lath nailing strips
for base, sides,
and front

11"

17½"

BASE

18"

19¾"

BACK

11¾"

SIDE

set strips ½" in
from edge

Step 5: *Mounting the magnetic catch*

Side view

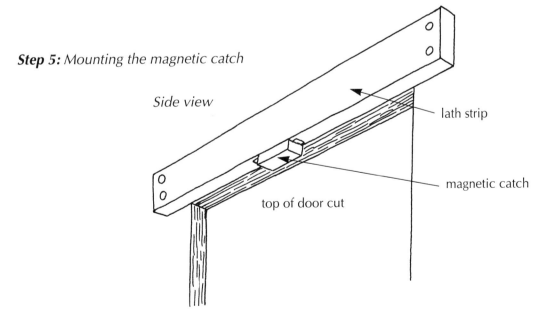

lath strip

magnetic catch

top of door cut

10. Cut eight pieces of ½" x 1¼" trim 11¾" long. Glue and nail these pieces to the four walls where they meet at their corners, overlapping the trim in the same direction as the wall pieces overlap.

11. Cut two pieces of ½" x 1¼" trim 16½" long. Glue and nail them to the bottoms of the side walls.

12. Cut one piece of ½" x1¼" trim 10¼" long. Glue and then nail this to the bottom of the back wall.

13. Cut two pieces of ½" x 1¼" trim 11¾" long. Using a miter box and its appropriate saw or a chop saw, cut the ends of these pieces at a 45° angle so they will be flush with the angle of the roof line when they are attached to the front and back walls. Attach these pieces of trim so that their longer edges rest on top of the vertical trim you've already attached to the front and back walls. The angle of the ends of the trim matches the angle of your barn's roof line.

MAKING THE WINDOWS

14. Locate a point 1" up from the trim on the bottom of one of your side walls and 1" in from the trim on the corner of the same side wall. Mark it with your pencil. Starting at this point, draw a line 3" long running parallel to the bottom trim. Go back to your starting point and draw a 4" line running parallel to the corner trim. These two lines represent the bottom and one of the sides of a window. Finish drawing the window by adding a line for the top and the second side. Repeat this process until you have two windows drawn on each side wall.

15. Paint the insides of your windows any color you desire.

16. Cut four pieces of scotia 3" long. Glue and nail them to the top edge of each window.

17. Cut eight pieces of parting bead 4" long and four pieces of parting bead 3" long. Attach the

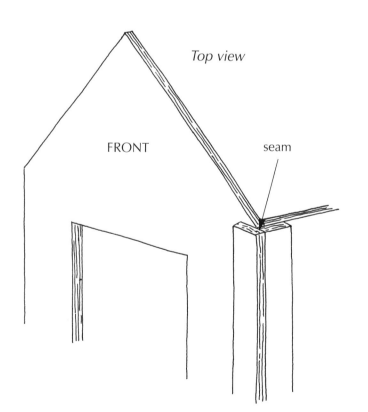

Step 10: Trim should overlap the same way as walls.

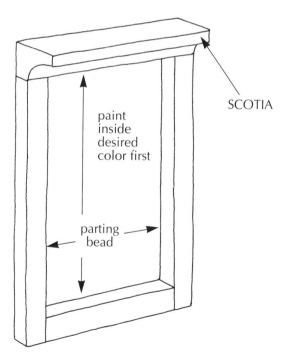

Steps 14–17: Use scotia or cove molding to create an overhang on top of your barn's windows.

4" pieces to the side edges of the windows and the 3" pieces to the bottom edges of the windows.

ATTACHING THE DOOR

18. Cut a piece of scotia 10¼" long. Glue and then nail it in line with the top of the cut out for the door.

19. Cut the plywood door down to 8½" x 6¼".

20. Attach hinges to the bottom of the door. Cut five pieces of ½" x 1¼" trim 8½" long. Glue and then nail them onto the door so that they cover the hinges.

FINISHING

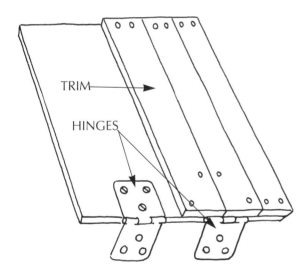

Step 20: When finished, the door's hinges should be sandwiched between the trim and the plywood door.

21. Do whatever painting, touch-up, and design you wish at this point. Refer to the color photo on page 7 for ideas, but feel free to use your own color scheme and decorating ideas.

22. Mount the metal pad from the magnetic catch onto the inside of the trim-covered door where it will meet the magnet.

23. Attach the wooden drawer pull to the outside of the door in the center about 1" from the top edge.

24. Attach the door's hinges to the base of the mailbox.

25. Paint the roof pieces. Lay them on the upper edges of the four walls of your barn mailbox. The two roof pieces should meet in a butt joint and the overhang should be even front and back.

26. Measure to find the middle of the 20" copper flashing. Using your pencil, draw a line down the center. Lay the straight edge of a board along this line and bend the flashing 90°.

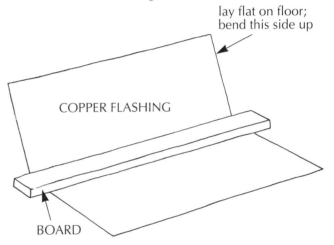

Step 26: Use a pine board laid across the copper flashing to get an even bend in the metal.

27. Tack the roofing copper onto the plywood roof. Round off the copper's corners with tin snips for safety.

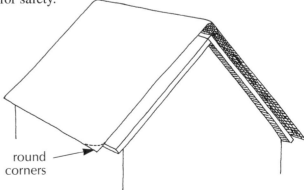

Step 27: Be sure to round off the corners of your copper roof for safety.

MOUNTING THE FLAG

28. To mount the flag, cut a block from a piece of scrap for the side of the barn. It should be wide enough so that the flag will clear the eaves when it is raised and lowered. For the flag, a simple 15-inch piece of 1" x 2" wood will do, painted any bright color but red so that it will stand out from the barn. Use a 2" lag bolt to mount the flag into the mounting block and barn about 4" from the barn's front edge. Twist it in tightly so that the flag stays upright after it has been raised. Regulations require the flag be on the right side of the mailbox when viewed from the front.

29. Coat all painted surfaces with polyurethane to protect your finished mailbox from the weather. Let everything dry for at least 36 hours.

FINISHING OPTIONS

MOUNTING
The New England Barn mailbox is best mounted on a support that extends the full length of the box. (See mounting diagrams on page 22).

MAINTENANCE
Coat painted surfaces with polyurethane once a year.

VARIATIONS
▶ The outside of the barn may be decorated with found objects.
▶ Instead of making windows, stencil your name and street number on the right side of the box.

House and Planter Mailbox

LEVEL: DIFFICULT

SEE COLOR PHOTO ON PAGE 6.

MATERIALS

For the House:

Government-approved, standard-size mailbox

¾" exterior plywood cut into:
    2 pieces 23¾" x 10¾", sides
    2 pieces 15¼" x 8⅝", front and back

½" exterior plywood cut into:
    2 pieces 29½" x 8½", roof

¼" plywood cut into:
    2 pieces 2" x 6", spacers

Various sizes of pine:

    2 pieces 2" x 2" x 3" pine, chimney
    1 piece 2" x 1¼" x 2¾" pine, flag spacer
    10 feet ½" x ³⁄₁₆" pine, window trim
    1 piece 3½" x 8" x ¼" pine, door
    1 piece ¾" x ¾" x 16" pine, inside brace or
       nailer for roof
    1 piece 1" x 2" x 15" pine, flag

For the Planter Boxes:

2 pieces flashing metal 19" x 17", boxes

4 pieces flashing metal 5½" x 4¾", planter ends

Exterior latex paint, your choice of colors for the
    house

2" lag bolt for the flag

Screws, sheet metal and wood

Nails

Waterproof glue

DESIGNED BY EDWARD SMITH, MARSHFIELD, VT

THIS BEAUTIFUL MAILBOX serves two purposes. It receives mail and it provides a wonderful space for more flowers. We recommend that you make a few holes in the bottom of the planter boxes for drainage and use a plastic liner in the metal box. If you put plants directly in the metal planter, the sun will overheat the roots of the plants.

Plants that drape over the sides look especially charming in the planter. Try trailing vinca, creeping phlox, alyssum, or thyme. Whatever you choose, this planter mailbox is sure to be noticed.

EQUIPMENT & TOOLS

Awl	Metal snips
C-clamps, optional	Paintbrushes
Chop saw or miter box and saw	Pencil
	Sandpaper
Drill	Screwdrivers
File	Speed square
Hammer	Table saw

MAKING THE HOUSE

1. Cut all the plywood to size.

2. Cut a 45° bevel on one of the long edges of both side pieces.

3. Cut a 45° bevel on one of the long edges of both roof pieces.

4. The roof of the house is a gable roof, which means it slopes down in two directions from the roof's center line. The angle of the roof is made by cutting gables, or triangles, in the top of the front and back pieces. To do this, hold the front and back pieces together so that one of the shorter sides is uppermost. Locate the exact center of this side. Using a speed square, draw two lines on a 45° angle from this center point on both the back and front pieces. Use a chop saw or miter box to cut these angles.

5. Once the gable cuts are done on both the front and back, draw a line on the front piece that separates the gable from the rest of the piece. Cut the front in two so that the gable is a separate piece.

6. Glue and then nail the two roof pieces together, using the ¾" x ¾" brace inside the peak to hold the two roof pieces together.

7. Glue and then nail the two side pieces to the back so that the beveled edges of the side pieces and the gable end of the back pieces are all uppermost.

8. Paint the various components of your house mailbox — the sides, front, back, roof, chimneys, and trim — to resemble the corresponding parts of an actual house, according to your own color scheme.

9. Draw and then paint in two windows on each side of the house. Once the paint is dry, cut pieces of painted trim to fit around the outside of the windows.

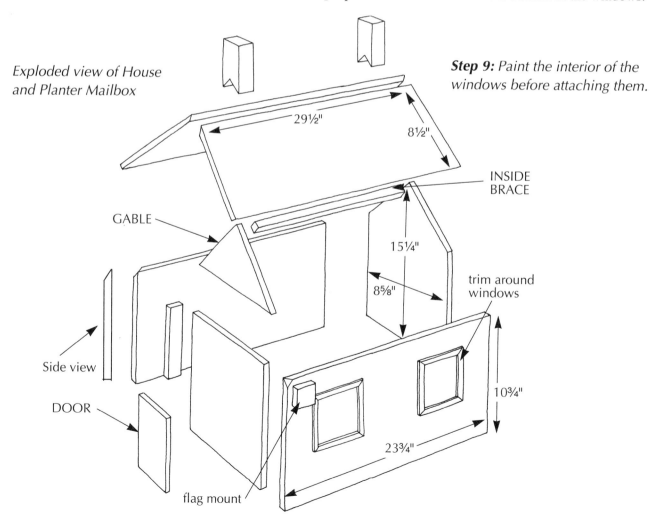

Exploded view of House and Planter Mailbox

Step 9: *Paint the interior of the windows before attaching them.*

29½"

8½"

INSIDE BRACE

GABLE

15¼"

8⅝"

trim around windows

Side view

DOOR

10¾"

23¾"

flag mount

10. Draw and then paint the door piece. Attach to the square front piece. Cut pieces of painted trim to fit around the outside of the door, if desired.

MAKING THE PLANTER BOXES

11. Lay out your flashing and use an awl to score the metal according to the measurements in the diagram below. Cut the pieces out with tin snips. The edges of flashing can be quite sharp, so be aware of your fingers.

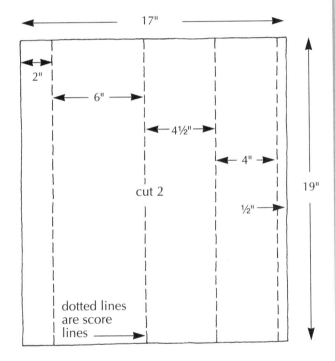

12. Unless you have a metal crimping tool, the best method to use to bend or crimp sheet metal is as follows:

▶ Locate two boards with straight edges at least 19" long. Taking one of the two pieces of flashing that will be used to make the body of the planter box, turn it so one of its 19" sides is toward you. Measure in ½" from the edge and score the metal along this line.

▶ Slide the flashing between the two pieces of board until the boards line up on the ½" mark. Only ½" of the flashing will be between the boards at this point.

▶ Clamp the two boards together or hold them tightly together while you bend the metal up and crease it.

▶ Turn the boards and flashing over so that the flashing is uppermost. In order to make the crease sharper, hammer the flashing where it is bent over one of the boards.

▶ Remove the boards and hammer the sheet metal over until it lays flat. This folding over of the flashing's edge will keep its sharpness away from your fingers.

You may use this same bending technique for all your sheet metal work even when the bend is only 90°. Check the illustrations below and shape the sheet metal into two boxes and four ends. To fold the end pieces for the planter boxes, follow the illustrations below.

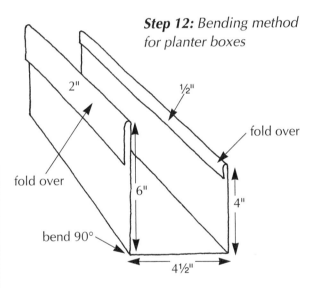

Step 12: *Bending method for planter boxes*

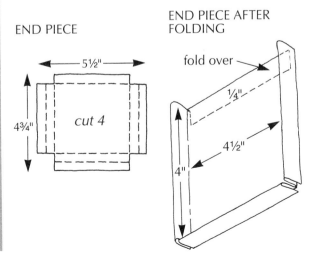

13. Once your flashing is crimped according to the illustrations, take one of the end pieces and turn it so that the folded edge of the crimps is facing you and the folded-over edge is uppermost. Slide this end onto the one of the open ends of a sheet metal box. (See illustration below.)

14. Fasten the end piece to the planter box by driving the point of a nail into the seam where the box and end come together. (See illustration below.) Drive the nail just until the metal on the opposite side of the nail begins to push out. It is easier to do this if you hold a small block of wood behind the metal into which you are driving the nail. Repeat this nailing process in two more places along this edge and in three places on each additional edge. Install the remaining three ends in the same way.

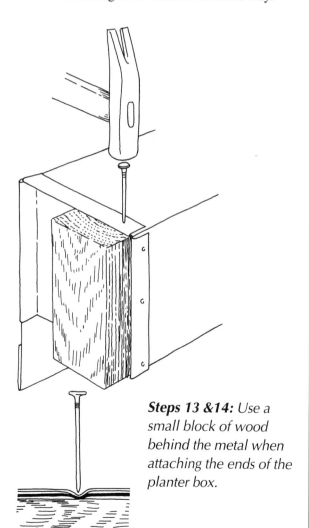

***Steps 13 &14:** Use a small block of wood behind the metal when attaching the ends of the planter box.*

ATTACHING THE PLANTER BOXES

15. Drill three equally spaced keyhole slots in the higher of the two sides of the planter box. The easiest way to make a keyhole slot is to drill a small hole just above a larger hole and file the metal between the two away.

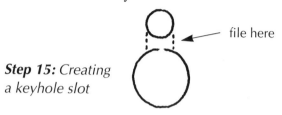

***Step 15:** Creating a keyhole slot*

FINAL ASSEMBLY

16. Glue and nail the chimneys to the roof.

17. Attach the front gable by screwing or nailing the peak of the gable into the roof brace on the front of the house. Then drive nails through the roof into the gable, at least three nails on each side of the roof.

18. Hold the planter box up to the side of the house so that the keyholes in the planter box are at least 1" up from the bottom edge of the side. The planter box should be located so that an equal amount of house shows on either side of the box. Using a pencil, mark the location of the upper part of the keyholes on the house.

19. Insert screws into these locations, leaving a tiny gap between the underside of the screw's head and the outer surface of the house's side. Panhead sheet metal screws, ¾", would work best here. Once you have hung the planter boxes from these screws, tighten the screws.

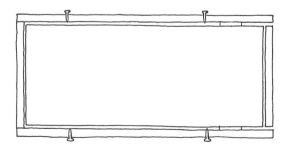

***Step 19:** Leave a small gap between the head of the screw and the house. Tighten after you attach the planter box.*

20. Place the house over the mailbox so that the center of the mailbox's latching mechanism matches the center of the bottom edge of the front gable. Using a pencil, mark the location of the latching mechanism on the bottom edge of the front gable.

21. Using a chisel or a jigsaw, cut a shallow notch in the bottom edge of the gable between the marks showing where the latching mechanism will rest.

22. Attach the house to the metal mailbox with sheet metal screws using plywood spacers near the front for door clearance. Attach the roof of the house to the mailbox with screws started from the inside of the mailbox.

23. Place the wooden front piece on the mailbox door as it will be attached. Using a pencil, mark the location of the mailbox's latching mechanism on the top edge of the front piece.

24. Using a chisel or a jigsaw, cut a shallow notch in the top edge of the front piece between the marks showing where the latching mechanism will rest.

25. Attach the front wall to the mailbox door with ¾" sheet metal screws, starting from the inside of the mailbox door, adjusting for side clearance, and making sure the notch in the front door matches the location of the latching mechanism.

MOUNTING THE FLAG

26. To mount the flag, cut a block from a piece of scrap for the side of the house. It should be wide enough so that the flag will clear the eaves when it is raised and lowered. For the flag, a simple 15-inch piece of 1" x 2" wood will do, painted any bright color. Use a 2" lag bolt to mount the flag into the mounting block and house about 4" from the house's front edge. Twist the bolt in tightly so that the flag stays upright after it has been raised. Regulations require the flag to be on the right side of the mailbox when viewed from the front.

FINISHING OPTIONS

MOUNTING
When plants, soil, and water are added to this mailbox, it will be heavy, so be sure you have a rugged mounting system available. If you do not already have a mounting mechanism in place, follow the instructions on page 26 to put a mailbox post made of 4" x 4" x 6' pressure-treated lumber into the ground.

MAINTENANCE
Repaint the house mailbox as needed. Remove the planter boxes at the end of each growing season.

VARIATIONS
▶ Paint your house mailbox to resemble your house.
▶ Instead of windows, add a nameplate or paint your name on the right side of the house mailbox as you view it from the street.

Seaside Lighthouse

LEVEL: DIFFICULT

SEE COLOR PHOTO ON PAGE 4.

MATERIALS

Government-approved, standard-size mailbox

Two pieces 1" x 12" x 8' pieces of pine*, cut into:

   One piece 6" x 17½", baseboard

   One piece 11¼" x 20½", floor

   Two pieces 9¼" x 13", cottage sides

   One piece 7" x 18", roof

   One piece 7¾" x 18", roof

   Three pieces, triangles with 9" base and 6½" sides, roof supports

   One piece, 11" diameter circle, top floor

   One piece, 9" diameter circle, tower railing

   Three pieces, 7 or 7½" diameter circles, tower nailers

   Three pieces, 3 or 3½" diameter circles, upper tower nailers

   Lighthouse siding strips, various lengths, 1½" wide

   Trim pieces, various lengths, ¾" wide, ripped at ½" thick

Eight pieces of ¼" dowel, each 4½" long

White cedar shingles (about 20)

Portion of light fixture for tower

Copper strip, aluminum flashing, or coffee can

Small box (1 lb) of 6d galvanized finish nails

Small box (1 lb) 4d galvanized finish nails

¾" galvanized small nails or ¾" roofing nails

Assortment of screws, 2", 1½"

Weatherproof glue

Exterior paintable caulk (water soluble preferable to silicone)

Paint (oil or exterior latex) black, white, dark red
Primer

(*Pine that's rough on one side is less costly than pine that's smooth on two sides, but rough-one-side is ⅞", rather than ¾", thick.)

DESIGNED BY KATHE MOTTOR, EASTHAMPTON, MA

INTRIGUED BY THE ROMANCE of the stately lighthouses lining the coast? Create a memorable replica of this beloved architecture for your mailbox.

EQUIPMENT & TOOLS

C-clamps	Nail set
Chop saw (optional)	Paintbrushes
Compressor and brad nailer (optional)	Sander (preferably orbital) with 80-120 grit sandpaper
Dremel (optional)	
Electric drill	Speed square or similar device to draw angles and straight lines
Hammer	
Jigsaw	
Measuring tape	Table saw, circular saw, or radial arm saw
Metal snips	

This project requires some prior knowledge of power tools and carpentry. You have two options for the lighthouse towers. You can purchase hollow porch posts at your local recycling or building salvage yard. Or you can construct the tower from scratch. Read through all the directions before making your decision.

CUTTING AND ASSEMBLING THE LIGHTHOUSE

1. If you decide to purchase hollow porch posts for this project, you need one with a 9" base and one with a 5" base. If you choose to make the towers, go to step 2. If you buy the towers, go to step 11.

2. If you chose rough-one-side pine as your building material, cut out three nailer circles of 7" diameter each. If you are using smooth-both-sides pine, your circles will be 7½" diameter. Don't worry about being right on the money with these dimensions — it's more important to get three circles the same size. These circles are the top, middle, and bottom nailers for the lower tower.

3. Cut four strips out of one of your 8' pine boards to a finished width of 1½" with a 10° bevel on both sides (see illustration below).

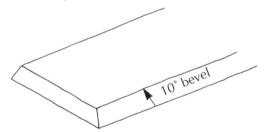

Step 3: Cut a 10° bevel on both sides of the strips you will use to make the outside of the tower.

4. Cut the four strips into 15 pieces of 21" each. There will be approximately 12" of waste.

5. Glue and then nail (using 4d finish nails) the first strip to the bottom, middle (at least 10" above the bottom), and top nailing circles. The narrower side of the strip will be touching the nailing circles and the wider (1½") side of the strip will be on the outside.

6. Glue and then nail a second strip to the nailing circles so that one of the outside edges of the first strip touches one of the outside edges of the second strip. The inside edges will have gaps between them.

7. Continue to the third piece. When you add the third piece, angle nail a 4d nail through the side of the third piece into the second about halfway down between circles. This helps prevent the pieces from twisting when in the weather.

8. When you are about halfway through this process, slide the back of the mailbox in between the bottom and middle nailing circles. Cut your strips to the appropriate lengths so that there will be space left open to accommodate the mailbox. The last strip will probably have to be ripped again to fit.

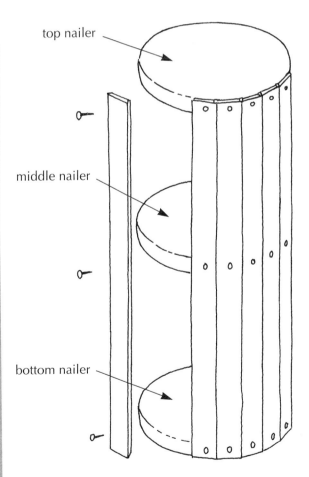

Steps 5–7: Glue and nail strips so that outside edges touch.

9. The 5" diameter tower is built in the same manner using two 3" circles if using rough-one-side pine or 3½" circles for smooth-both-sides pine. In this case, the strips you cut will be 12" in height (use the waste from cutting the first set of strips if you can). You will need 11 strips for this tower.

10. Sand the ridges on the outside of the tower smooth and fill in the cracks with filler. When the filler dries, sand the towers again until they are smooth and round. Prime and paint white.

IF YOU PURCHASE POSTS FOR THE LIGHTHOUSE

11. Using a circular saw, cut a 21" section from the 9½" diameter hollow post. Cut the 5" diameter post to 12". Place the back of the mailbox against the 9½" diameter post and trace the outline of the box onto the post (see illustration below). Using a

jigsaw, cut out this outline, leaving enough room for the mailbox to easily slide in and out. If your jigsaw has the capability to cut at an angle, cut the outline out at approximately a 10° angle.

12. Center the larger post (this is the bottom section of the tower) on one end of the floorboard with the mailbox opening facing toward the rest of the floor. Glue and nail in place (see illustration below).

MAKING THE LIGHTHOUSE KEEPER'S COTTAGE

13. Cut a 10° angle on one of the short ends of both the side pieces of what will be the lighthouse keeper's cottage. Take the two sides of the keeper's cottage and place them on the floorboard 1" in from each side with the angled end fitted against the tower (see illustration below). Glue and then nail in place.

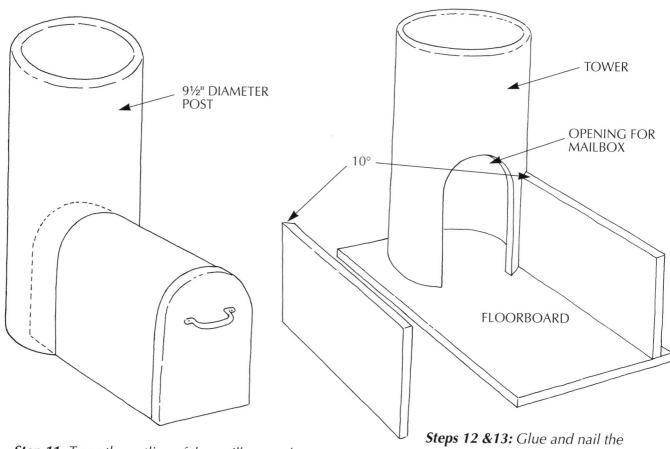

Step 11: Trace the outline of the mailbox on the 9½" diameter post.

Steps 12 &13: Glue and nail the post to the floorboard, with the opening facing toward the far end.

14. Attach the three roof supports (also called gables because of their angled sides) to the sides, one flush with the front, one in the middle, and one against the tower. (See illustration.)

15. Slide the mailbox through the keeper's cottage and into the lighthouse. Make sure it can slip easily in and out. If it doesn't, make your adjustments now.

16. Attach the roof sections. Place the first, smaller section flush with the tops of the gables (see illustration). Glue and then nail it in place.

17. Where the two roof sections meet, the second roof section overlaps the first. Glue and then nail it into place.

SHINGLING THE ROOF

18. Now it's time to add the white cedar shingles to the roof. Decide what you think looks good (see color photo page 4 for ideas) and cut the shingles to length.

19. Start your first row at the tower. Place the first piece against the tower and scribe the curve of the tower onto the shingle and cut it out so that it fits snugly against the tower. Any gaps can be filled in later with caulk. Glue and then nail this piece in place.

20. Continue shingling, working from the tower to the front of the keeper's cottage. Leave at least a ¾" overhang at the front to allow for a ½" trim board.

21. Repeat this shingling process for the other side, making the shingles flush at the ridge of the roof. If you decide to add a second layer of shingles, make them about a third the length of the first layer and repeat the process starting at the tower. Remember to overlap the joints of the shingle below by at least an inch (see illustration).

22. If you don't have a piece of copper sheet or aluminum flashing for the roof cap, you can cut a 2" strip from a coffee can. Measure the ridge of the roof and cut your 2" copper sheet, flashing, or coffee can strip to the same length.

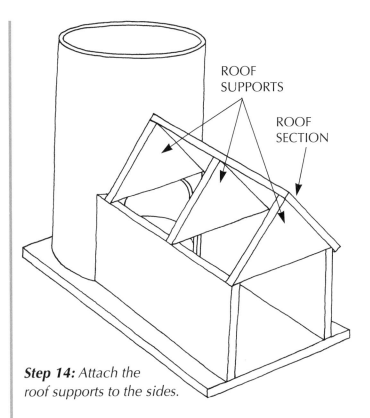

ROOF SUPPORTS

ROOF SECTION

Step 14: Attach the roof supports to the sides.

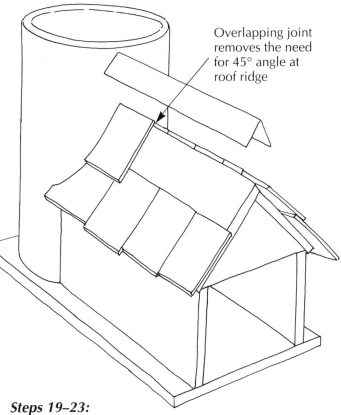

Overlapping joint removes the need for 45° angle at roof ridge

Steps 19–23:
Leave a ¾" overhang of shingles at the front of the lighthouse keeper's cottage.

23. Scribe a line 1" down from the ridge along the length of the roof. Nail the long edge of the metal strip along this line. Bend the overhanging part over the ridge and nail it in place.

FINISHING

24. Trim the corners, base, and gable eaves of the keeper's cottage with strips of pine ½" wide. I used trim around the edges of the floorboard as well. The trim will help close any gaps that there may be between the tower and rear of the cottage (see illustration below).

25. Caulk to fill in any gaps along the side and roof where the tower meets the cottage.

26. To make the railing for the upper part of the tower, take the 9" circle you cut from one of the pine boards. Locate its center point and draw a 6" circle within the 9" circle using the same center. There should be a 1½" margin all around the outside of the 9" circle. Cut out the 6" circle (see illustration) so that you have a ring.

27. With your pencil, lay out where the baluster dowels will go in the ring by locating eight points centered and equidistant around the ring (see illustration). There's no need to be exact — just estimate what looks good.

28. Center the railing ring in the 11" circle. Clamp them together and drill out the ¼" baluster holes you marked on the top. Drill through both pieces. Make a pencil mark at one point on the two pieces where they join to help line them up after you unclamp them.

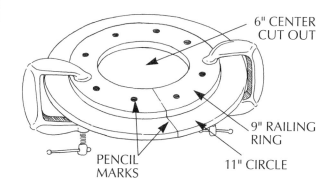

Steps 26–27: Clamp circles together and drill through both pieces.

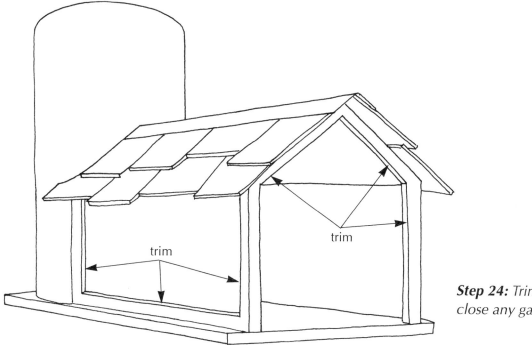

Step 24: Trim will help close any gaps.

29. Take your 4½" dowel pieces and place them in the holes so that they are flush with the top and bottom. To reinforce the structure and help it withstand heavy weather, add four pieces of the 10° angled strips you used to form the towers, cut to fit between the ring and 11" circle. These support posts should be centered between the balusters (see illustration). Glue and then nail the support posts in place. Glue the dowels in place. When the glue is dry, you can sand the top of the ring smooth.

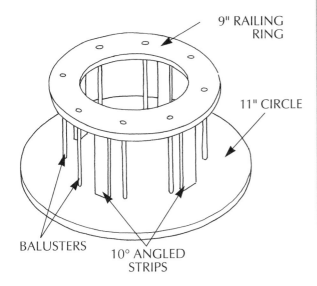

9" RAILING RING

11" CIRCLE

BALUSTERS

10° ANGLED STRIPS

Step 29: Evenly space the supports between the balusters. Glue and nail in place.

PAINTING

30. Take the time to prime and paint the railing assembly with two coats of black paint. Prime and paint the upper tower section white at this time and do whatever decorative painting you want before attaching the tower section to the railing assembly (see color photo page 4 for ideas).

31. When the painted pieces are dry, center the 5" tower piece on the 11" circle and apply glue to the bottom of the tower. Let the two pieces adhere for a moment then turn the whole piece over and nail through the bottom of the railing floor section into the bottom of the tower. (If you bought the tower, you may want to fix a block of wood in its center by driving nails through the post into the block in at least four places. This will give you more surface to nail the rail assembly to than just the outer rim of the post.)

32. Cut the remaining 10° angled strips to decorate the base tower. They can run from the top to the bottom or be a miserly 2". Decide what you like for your tower (see color photo page 4 for ideas). I usually add an even number — 4, 6, or 8 strips — evenly spaced around the top, as if supporting the railing assembly. Prime and paint these pieces black before attaching them to the tower. You can touch them up after they are glued and nailed in place.

FINAL ASSEMBLY AND DECORATION

33. Attach the upper tower to the lower tower as follows: Apply a layer of paintable caulk to the top of the lower tower. Place the upper unit onto the lower unit and center it. Nail or screw the upper unit to the bottom unit.

34. If you found a suitable light fixture for the top of your lighthouse, you should paint it now and attach it to the top. Or you can make your own in any design that strikes your fancy.

35. Decorate the keeper's cottage to your liking. I've added doors and windows made from the scrap left over from building the project and used my Dremel to cut in shingle lines on the roof and sides of the cottage. It can also be left plain. Take the time to fill the nail holes, caulk any gaps, sand, and then start your painting. The lower tower is white, the keeper's cottage is white, the floorboard is black (painted both sides), the balusters, railing, and supports are black, the upper tower white, and the roof of the cottage red.

36. I bought a new baked-enamel mailbox to use inside the lighthouse cover. White or black is fine. Attach the 6" x 17½" baseboard to the bottom of the mailbox with screws through the holes along the sides of the lip of the mailbox. Make sure the board is flush with the back of the mailbox to allow enough room in the front to easily open and close the box. Slide the mailbox into the lighthouse cover. Leave about a 1" overhang to allow the door to open and shut properly. When you have the box centered, attach it to the lighthouse cover with four screws. Screw through the bottom of the cover up into the baseboard beneath the mailbox.

FINISHING OPTIONS

MOUNTING

You will need a sturdy post for this mailbox — at least a 4 x 4. A flat arm and no back is best. There are two ways to attach the mailbox.

▶ Remove the mailbox from the lighthouse cover. Place the lighthouse cover onto the post and decide where you want it. Using a pencil, mark the bottom of the cover along the edge of the post arm. Remove the lighthouse cover and drill several holes front to back between the lines you just drew. Place the lighthouse cover back on the post and attach it with screws through the holes you just drilled. Insert the mailbox back into the cover and replace the screws you use to attach the box to the lighthouse cover.

▶ Take a board slightly smaller than the lighthouse cover and attach it to the top of the post. Screw or nail it in place. Place the lighthouse cover on top of the board and attach it by screwing through the bottom of the board into the bottom of the lighthouse cover.

In all cases, open the mailbox and check to be sure no sharp screw tips are poking through the bottom of the mailbox. If so, file them flat.

MAINTENANCE

Your maintenance schedule will depend on what paint you chose, as well as weather and road conditions around your mailbox. Oil paint will last longer but takes longer to apply and clean up. Exterior latex will last around five years and is easy to apply and clean up.

Model A Ford

MATERIALS

Government-approved, standard-size mailbox, with removable flag

¼" plywood* cut into:
     2 pieces 20" x 13¼", sides

¾" plywood* cut into:
     1 piece 8⅛" x 12", front
     1 piece 12" x 8⅛,", top
     1 piece 8¾" x 8⅛", back
     1 piece 6⅛" x 18⅜", mounting plate
     5 circles 5" diameter, wheels

2" x 8" pine cut into:
     1 piece 3', curved section of top (transition pieces) and fenders

¾" pine cut into:
     2 pieces ⅞" x 10", spacers
     2 pieces 2¼" x 11⅜", running boards
     1 piece 8⅛" long, visor

5 stainless steel carriage bolts, 1½", with 7 nuts, 5 washers, for wheel mounts
Sandpaper
Nails
Screws
Flashing for windshield
Paint, exterior latex or other weatherproof paint
Waterproof glue
Half-round ⅜" molding for sides of cab (optional)

*Plywood used in this project should be exterior grade, good-one-side.

DESIGNED BY EDWARD SMITH, MARSHFIELD, VT

WHEN HENRY FORD decided to make the Model A, he made them all the same color because it was easier and less expensive that way. Now, you can paint your Model A mailbox all black if you wish but if there's a can of blue or yellow paint lying around, why not go Mr. Ford one better?

EQUIPMENT & TOOLS

Band saw (A bench-top 8-inch band saw is very handy for this project.)
C-clamps (optional)
Drill
Jigsaw
Plane
Sander or sandpaper
Screwdrivers
Square
Table saw, circular saw, or handsaw
Tin snips (optional)
Wrenches

This project calls for a bit of woodworking expertise and if you have access to a band saw, this project will be much easier. While you can cut circles with a jigsaw, it's a lot harder to get them round. If you're set on this Model A but can't get your hands on a band saw, check out the supply of wooden wheels in your local hobby shop.

CUTTING

1. Using measurements given in materials list, cut the back and top pieces from ¾" plywood using a table saw, circular saw, or handsaw.

2. Enlarge the size of the pattern pieces illustrated below using the directions and grid on pages 120–122.

3. Using a pencil, trace the outline of the pattern pieces of the side and front pieces on ¾" plywood. Using your band saw or jigsaw, cut the side and front pieces according to the patterns.

4. Cut pieces of 2" pine according to the pattern for the fenders below, and on page 79 for the transition pieces between the top and back.

Cutting Diagram

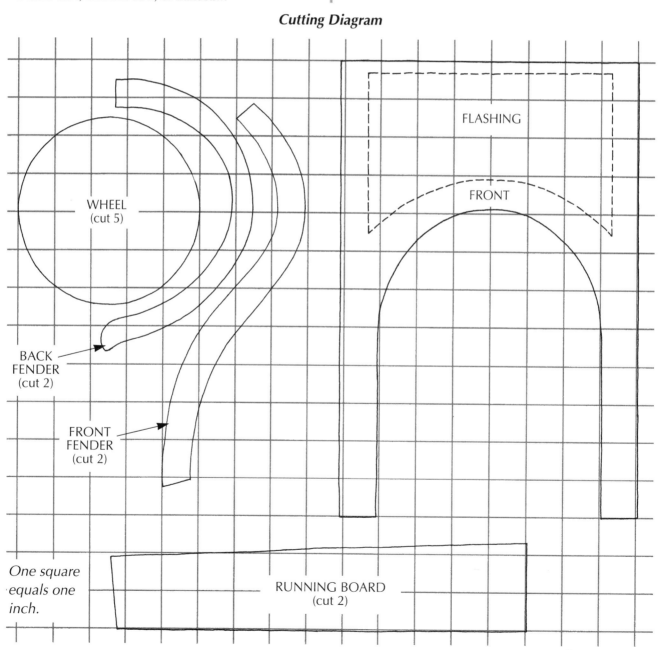

WHEEL
(cut 5)

FLASHING

FRONT

BACK
FENDER
(cut 2)

FRONT
FENDER
(cut 2)

RUNNING BOARD
(cut 2)

One square equals one inch.

Cutting Diagram

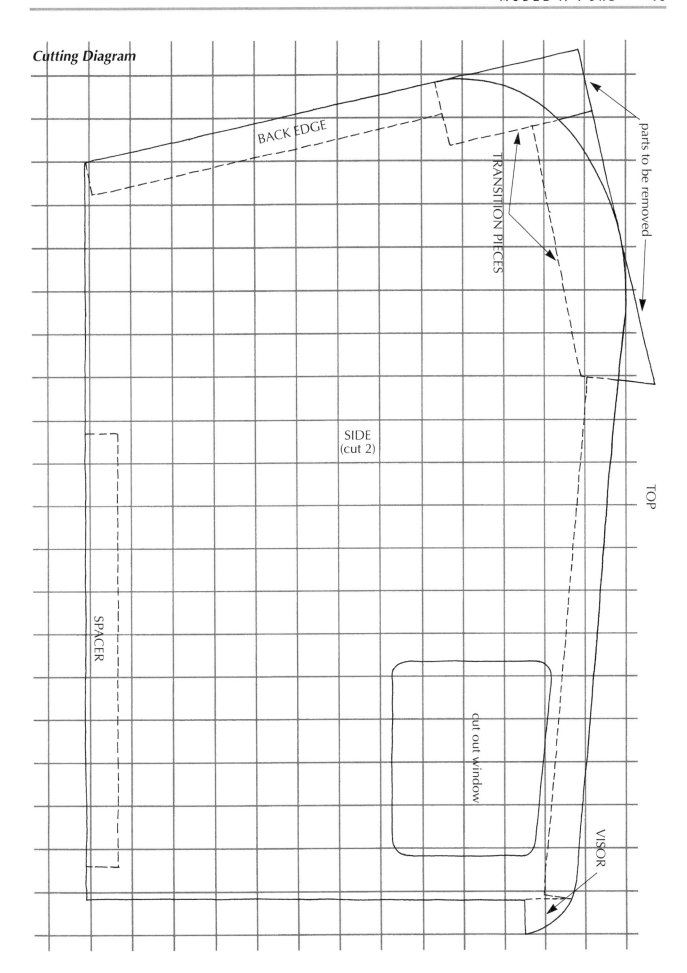

BACK EDGE

TRANSITION PIECES

parts to be removed

SIDE
(cut 2)

TOP

SPACER

cut out window

VISOR

ASSEMBLING

5. Temporarily tack or clamp all the parts together. Mark the pine pieces to fit, including the visor, then shape them by whatever method is best for you. (I used a plane and sander.)

6. Glue and then nail the cab pieces together, including the spacers and visor.

7. Sand the cab smooth.

PAINTING

8. Using exterior latex or other weatherproof paint, paint the cab of the Model A. Refer to the color photo on page 8 for ideas. Oil-based paints work just as well as latex but they take longer to dry and the cleanup is messier.

9. Using masking tape and newspaper, cover the mailbox's door and the first ½" of the front. These areas will become the radiator and grill of the Model A. Paint the rest of the mailbox to match your Model A.

FINAL ASSEMBLY

10. Using a band saw, cut the wheels and fenders according to the pattern illustrated on page 78. Once they are cut, trim the running boards to match the pattern. Sand and paint the wheels and running board.

11. Mount the rear wheels to the side pieces with carriage bolts. Mount the spare wheel to the back with a carriage bolt.

12. Attach the rear fenders with screws, working from the inside of the cab.

13. Glue and then screw the running boards to the underside of the cab, flush with the spacers on the inside of the side pieces. The screws should go through the running board and into the spacers with the front of the rear fenders sitting atop the running board.

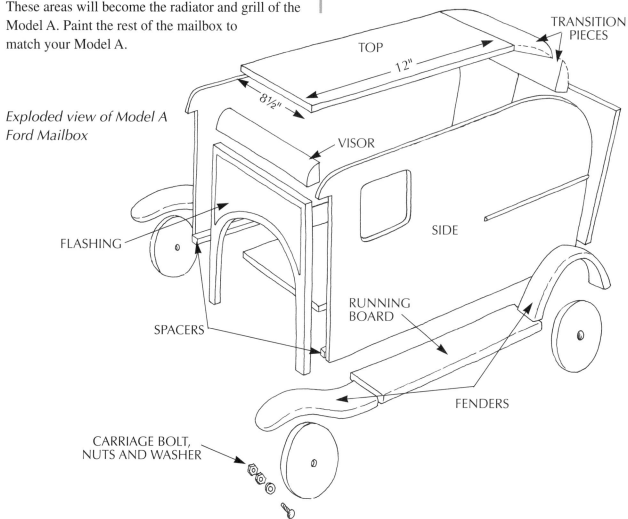

Exploded view of Model A Ford Mailbox

14. Paint the front door and first ½" of the mailbox to represent the grill of a Model A. See color photo on page 8.

15. Remove the flag and flag holder from the right side of the mailbox. Be sure to keep all the pieces together.

16. Insert the mailbox into the cab, allowing approximately 8¼" to project from the cab. Working from inside the mailbox's lower lip, screw lip of the box into the spacers.

17. Mark the placement of the front fenders on the mailbox. When they are attached, the rear of the front fenders should butt up to the running boards. Note where the mailbox door will be in contact with the front fenders and notch the front of the fenders for clearance for the door.

18. With your electric drill, drill screw holes through the mailbox where the fenders will be attached. Attach the front fenders with screws started from inside the box.

19. Attach the front wheels to the lip on the base of the mailbox with carriage bolts. Use an extra nut inside the front wheels to space them away from the mailbox door.

20. Cut a piece of flashing to fit the upper part of the front piece. This represents the Model A's windshield. Nail the flashing to the front of the cab.

21. Attach the flag to the right side (as you're facing the mailbox from the street) of the Model A. Use a small block of pine as a spacer so that the flag will not rub up against the paint of the mailbox.

FINISHING OPTIONS

MOUNTING
Cut a 6⅛" x 18⅜" mounting plate from ¾" plywood for your Model A. Notch the mounting plate to clear the front-wheel mounting bolts. Screw the plywood mounting plate to your wooden mailbox post so that at least one-third of the plywood sits behind the post. This will help balance the weight of your finished mailbox. Additional bracing from the box mounting plate to the post is recommended — this is a heavy box.

Attach the box to the mounting plate using the exposed holes in the mailbox.

MAINTENANCE
Repaint your mailbox as needed. Exterior latex paint should last approximately five years.

VARIATION
Paint your Model A in colors of your choice. If you choose red, repaint the mailbox flag another bright color so that it will stand out from your mailbox.

Big Yellow School Bus

LEVEL: MODERATE TO DIFFICULT

SEE COLOR PHOTO ON PAGE 7.

MATERIALS

Government-approved, standard-size mailbox
    with removable flag

1   sheet ¾" exterior-grade plywood, 4' x 2',
    good one side, cut into:
      2 pieces, 19½" x 13½", sides
      2 pieces, 13½" x 8", front and back
      1 piece, 19½" x 6½", top
      1 piece, 8" x 2", bottom rear filler

1   piece 1" x 6" pine (No. 2 grade), 3' long,
    cut into:
      2 pieces, 8" x 1½", bumpers
      4 circles, each 5" diameter, wheels
      1 piece, 2¼" x 2¼", spacer for flag mount

1   piece ¾" thick plywood or pine cut into
    17½" x 6⅛", base

1   piece ¼" exterior-grade plywood, large
    enough to cut four 3"-diameter circles, for
    wheel centers

18 pieces ⅜" wooden screw plugs, for lights

Waterproof wood glue

14 flathead #6 wood screws, 1¼"

1   round-head #6 wood screw, 1¼"

2   #6 sheet metal screws, ⅝"

1½" finish nails

Stencil with ⅜"– ¾" letters and numbers

Wood filler

Sandpaper

Exterior primer

Exterior trim black paint

Exterior trim yellow paint

White gloss craft paint

Red gloss craft paint

Amber gloss craft paint

DESIGNED BY JOE DE JULIO, M & J'S WOODCRAFTERS,
WATERVLIET, NY

THIS IS A GREAT PROJECT FOR SOMEONE with a
bit of woodworking experience. Cutting the
wheels for your Big Yellow School Bus is easiest on a band saw but if you don't have one sitting on your work bench, don't despair. Circles
can be cut with a jigsaw. Or you might want to
check out the wooden wheel selection at your
local hobby shop for substitutes.

One of the benefits of a mailbox dressed like
a yellow school bus is that it will show up
against a backdrop of snow.

EQUIPMENT & TOOLS

Circular saw or handsaw
Drill
File (optional)
Hammer
Saber saw, jigsaw, or band saw
Screwdriver
Table saw

CUTTING

1. Lay out and cut all pieces of wood as described in the materials list.

2. As you build this project, be sure to keep the rough side of the plywood on the inside of the school bus. Measure 18" from the front edge on the rough side of both your side pieces and draw a line parallel with the short side of the piece at this point. Cut a groove along this line ⅛" wide x ¼" deep for the rear seam of the mailbox.

3. Mark the curves where the front and back wheels will show on the side pieces. Cut arcs in the side pieces for wheel wells.

4. Mark and drill ⅜" holes in the front and rear pieces for the screw plugs, which will represent the bus's flashing red and amber lights.

5. Lay the back end of the mailbox on the front piece so that the mailbox is centered and the bottoms are flush with one another. Cut this archway out and be sure the mailbox will slide in and out easily.

6. File or sand all of the wheels' edges to round them off like tires.

PAINTING

7. Use an exterior wood filler to fill all the voids in the plywood's edges. Sand and paint all pieces as shown in the illustrations. Start with an exterior primer, and use an exterior house trim paint for the finish coat. A second finish coat of paint can be applied after you assemble all the body pieces. This will allow you to fill in and sand over any joints or nail holes.

8. Paint the mailbox door and the portion of the mailbox that will protrude from the body of the bus yellow to match your school bus.

9. Using your craft paint, paint eight of the wooden screw plugs red, eight amber, and two white.

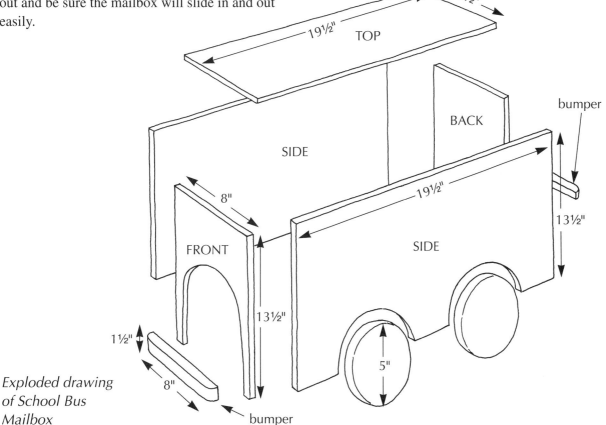

Exploded drawing of School Bus Mailbox

ASSEMBLING

10. Apply glue to one long edge of the roof piece. Nail one side piece onto the roof piece, making sure the roof's glued edge is flush with the top of the side piece. Glue and nail the other side piece onto the roof in the same way.

11. Nail the front and back ends of the bus onto the roof and side assembly.

12. Glue and nail the 2" fill piece at the bottom of the rear piece.

13. Screw the wood base liner into the bottom recess of the mailbox, making sure the mailbox door can open and close freely. Remove the flag and flag holder from the mailbox. Make sure you keep all the pieces together.

14. Place the bus assembly over the mailbox and secure them together with #6 1¼" flathead screws, working from inside the mailbox.

15. Drill and countersink holes in the center of the four wheels for screws. Center wheels in the

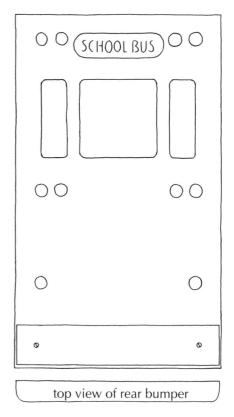

top view of rear bumper

School bus back view

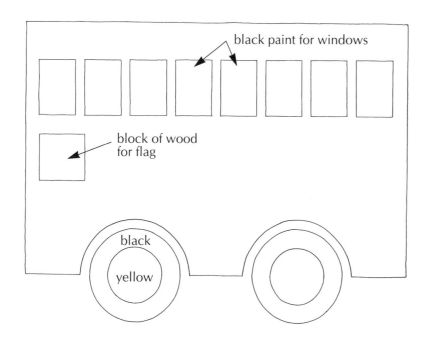

black paint for windows

block of wood for flag

black

yellow

School bus side view

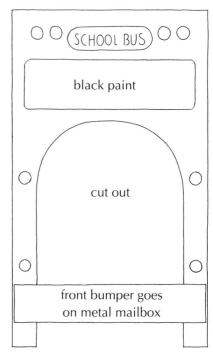

SCHOOL BUS

black paint

cut out

front bumper goes on metal mailbox

School bus front view

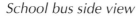

wheel wells so that the hole in the center of the wheel is located over the lip of the mailbox. Mark the location of all the wheel holes on the mailbox lip, remove the wheels, and drill holes through the lip of the metal box. Fasten the wheels in place with screws through the wheels, metal lip and into the wood liner.

16. Glue and nail the wheel centers onto the wheels.

17. Screw the rear bumper to the school bus assembly. Working from inside the mailbox's door, use sheet metal screws to attach the front bumper.

18. Glue the painted red, amber, and white lights into their predrilled holes.

FINISHING

19. Glue and nail the flag spacer block to the right side of the mailbox as you face it from the road. Attach the flag to the block with screws through its center.

20. Use your stencil to paint whatever markings you choose on the bus. This could be your name or the name of your local school. Touch up the paint where it's needed.

FINISHING OPTIONS

MOUNTING
The wood liner in the mailbox bottom allows mounting to a wooden or metal post. For wooden posts, use 1½" angle irons and screws to make attachment of the mailbox easy. A pipe flange can be used for a metal post.

MAINTENANCE
If you live in an area where snowplows are hazardous to the health of your mailbox, it might be wise to save your old mailbox and put it out when the white stuff begins to fly. If you put a wood liner in the bottom of your old box, you'll be able to make a quick seasonal change.
Touch up the paint as needed.

VARIATION
Check the school buses in your district for any special markings. It's easy to make your mailbox resemble them.

E*arth-Moving Bulldozer*

LEVEL: MODERATE

SEE COLOR PHOTO ON PAGE 8.

MATERIALS

Government-approved, standard-size black
mailbox with removable flag

1 sheet ¾" exterior grade plywood, good one
   side, 2' x 4', cut into:
    2 pieces, 16½" x 21", sides
    1 piece, 6⅜" x 10", cab front
    1 piece, 6⅜" x 6¾", cab rear
    2 pieces, 6⅜" x 4¼", cab top and cab
    floor
    1 piece, 6⅜" x 6¼", rear hood
    1 piece, 6⅜" x 9¾", rear

1 sheet ¼" lauan plywood, 2' x 2', cut into:
    20 circles, 2½" in diameter, track wheels
    1 piece, 11" x 5", plow
    1 piece, 6⅜" x 2", seat back

2 pieces of 2" x 4" pine, free of large knots, each
   26" long, tracks
1 piece of 2" x 2", about 5½" long, plow mount
1 piece 1¼" cove molding, 11" long, bottom
   curve of plow
1 piece pine, ¾" x 1½" x 3", exhaust housing
1 piece ⅜" dowel, 2½" long, exhaust pipe
1 piece ¾" plywood or pine, 17½" x 6¼",
   mailbox base
Waterproof wood glue
48 flathead screws, #6 x 1¼" (multi-use drywall
   screws will work)
6 flathead wood screws, #6 x ¾"
3 sheet metal screws, 1" long
1" brads, optional
Wood filler
Exterior primer paint
Black, yellow, and silver exterior trim paint
Sandpaper

DESIGNED BY JOE DE JULIO, M & J'S WOODCRAFTERS,
WATERVLIET, NY

PLYWOOD COMMONLY COMES in 4' x 8' sheets
but many lumber yards now carry quarter sheets
(the size you need for this project) of this standard building material. So check around to
determine whether your local supplier carries
this size.

    If you're just starting out as a woodworker,
this would be a good project for you. A small
drill press would be helpful for this mailbox but
it isn't necessary.

EQUIPMENT & TOOLS

Circular saw, table saw, or handsaw
Drill press with a circle cutter (optional)
Drill with a 2½" Fostner bit
Files
Hammer
Hole saw
Saber saw, jigsaw, or scroll saw
Screwdriver

1. Lay out and cut all pieces of wood as shown below.

cab front	cab rear	rear	rear hood	cab top	cab floor
side			side		

2. Using the patterns on page 88, cut the cab's front, rear, and sides as shown.

3. Turn the side pieces so that the rough side of the wood is facing you. Measure in 17¾" from the front edge of each piece and draw a line parallel with the back edge at this point. Cut grooves along this line ⅛" wide x ¼" deep for the rear seam of the bulldozer.

4. Use a circle cutter or hole saw to cut 20 discs, 2½" in diameter, from the ¼" lauan plywood. These are the wheels that will be set into the tracks.

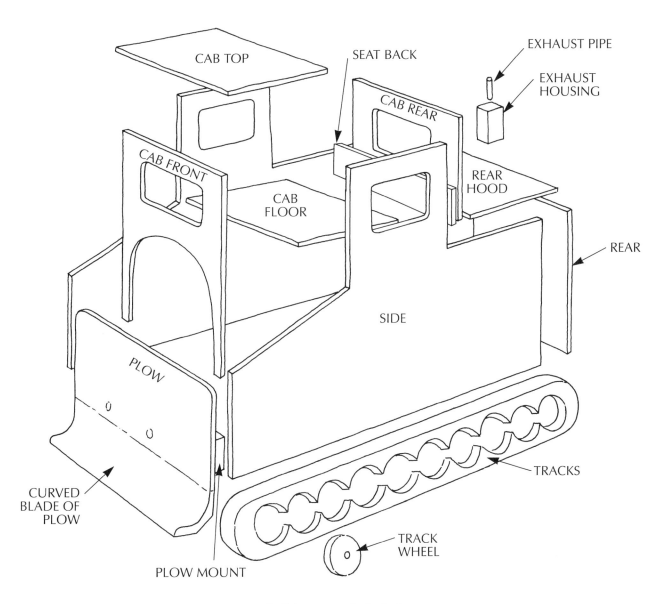

Bulldozer exploded view

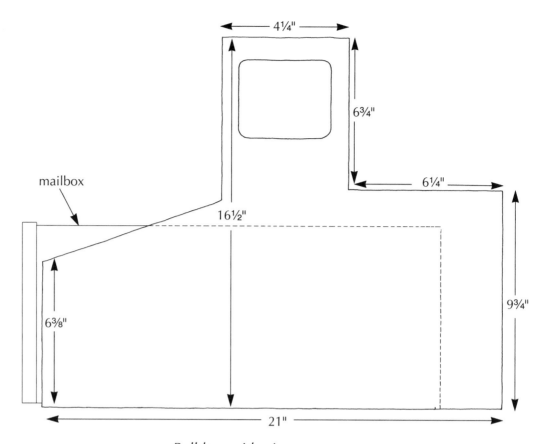

Bulldozer side view

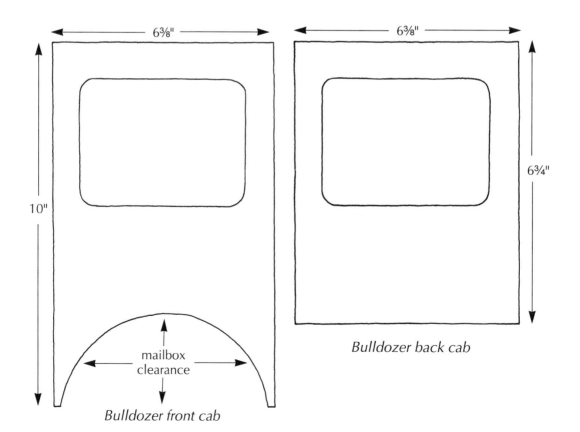

Bulldozer front cab

Bulldozer back cab

5. Mark the center line of each 2" x 4" x 26" piece of pine (the tracks). Center and mark ten adjoining circles along this line so that they are just touching each other.

6. Drill out the marked circles to about ½" depth. A Fostner bit, like the ones used to drill large holes for door locks, works best. Round off the front and back ends of the tracks.

7. Glue the piece of cove molding to the bottom of the ¼" plywood plow. This can be reinforced with 1" brads hammered through the cove molding into the plywood after you have carefully drilled pilot holes.

PAINTING

8. Use exterior wood filler to fill all the voids in the plywood's edges and face. Allow it to dry, then file and sand all the pieces smooth where necessary.

9. Prime all the pieces with an exterior primer. Don't forget the front 12" of the mailbox itself, along with the mailbox door. Apply one coat of exterior finish paint. The body pieces, including the flag spacer, plow pieces, and lauan discs should be yellow. The track pieces and seat back should be black. The exhaust housing and pipe can be black or silver.

ASSEMBLING

10. Screw or nail the exhaust housing in place on the rear hood piece. Drill a ⅜" hole about ½" deep into the top of the housing, toward the back. Glue the piece of dowel (exhaust pipe) into place.

11. Glue, clamp, and screw the cab front, back, and floor between the side pieces as shown on page 88. Then glue, clamp, and screw the cab top on. Countersink all the screw heads so they are flush with the surface of the wood.

12. Screw the wooden base piece into the bottom recess of the mailbox, drilling holes through the bottom lip of the box. Place the bulldozer's body assembly over the mailbox and secure it with four #6 x 1¼" flathead screws.

13. Screw the bulldozer tracks to the sides of the bulldozer body. The tracks should extend 1¼" below the bulldozer's sides and 2¾" from the rear of the body.

14. Glue the yellow wheel discs into the recesses in the tracks. Now screw each disc in place with a wood screw through its center. Use shorter, ¾" wood screws for the front and rear discs on each side so that the screw tips will not protrude through the back of the tracks.

MOUNTING THE FLAG

15. Remove the flag assembly from the mailbox. Be sure to keep all the parts together. Glue and nail the flag spacer block to the right side (as you view it from the road) of the bulldozer's body for the flag assembly. Screw the flag in place.

FINISHING

16. Screw the plow piece onto its 2" x 2" mounting piece. The mounting piece should be centered 2½" down from the top of the plow.

17. Drill three holes in the mailbox door to match placement of the plow assembly. Screw the plow assembly to the front of the mailbox with sheet metal screws through these three holes. The bottom edge of the plow should be slightly higher than the bottom of the track assembly.

18. Glue the seat back into the bulldozer's cab.

19. Apply finish coats of paint where necessary.

FINISHING OPTIONS

MOUNTING

This is a heavy box. The wood liner in the mailbox bottom allows mounting to a wooden or metal post, which should be centered directly under the bulldozer's cab. If you are using a wooden post, 1½" angle irons and screws make it easy to attach the mailbox to the post. A pipe flange can be used for a pipe post.

MAINTENANCE

In areas where snowplows are a hazard, save your old box for snow season use. Put a wood liner in its bottom to allow for quick seasonal changes.

Repaint as necessary.

VARIATION

Dress up your box with decals or trim lines to suit your taste. Your name and house number can be incorporated into this design.

Autumn Sky

LEVEL: EASY

SEE COLOR PHOTO ON PAGE 15.

MATERIALS

Government-approved, standard-size mailbox or a wooden mailbox of the same size

Spray primer*

Spray paint (spray enamel in flat white and harbor blue used in this project)

Clear finish

Block printing inks and vehicle, the smallest tubes available

Palette (window or picture-frame glass or a disposable foam dinner plate)

Ink mixers (1" x 2" scraps of mat board or a palette knife)

Ink applicators:
available in all shapes and sizes. You can use artists' flat-bristle brushes or a dauber made with ¼" foam padding cut into a 3" circle and secured with a rubber band over a bottle cork.

Sandpaper, wet or dry 220 grit

Newsprint

Leaves

*I recommend Premium Rust-oleum Auto Primer, Premium Rust-oleum Spray Enamel, and Premium Rust-oleum Clear Finish for priming, painting, and finishing. Remember that this mailbox is going to be out in the sun, snow, rain, and gloom of night so you want to be sure that whatever products you choose can withstand the elements.

DESIGNED BY LAURA DONNELLY BETHMANN, TUCKERTON, NJ

AUTUMN IS MY FAVORITE SEASON, and I especially enjoy the colorful dance of gracefully falling leaves. This decorated mailbox is a simple project made with materials that are available at art, craft, and hardware stores. Newsprint is available in pads from art stores, but if you have a local newspaper that prints its own editions, stop by and ask if they have the end of a roll you can buy.

Before you begin, explore around your house for leaves with interesting shapes. Or perhaps your area is well-known for a certain tree, bush, or fern. Samples of the foliage from these plants could decorate this mailbox.

EQUIPMENT & TOOLS

Drafting tape

Tweezers

PREPARING THE SURFACE

1. You can nature print your existing metal or wood mailbox. A friend gave me an old rural mailbox, which had been sitting outside near the chicken coop for quite a while. The paint was chipped in places and the metal exposed, but the only rust was on the door hinge. I washed it inside and out with mild soap and water, then left it outdoors to dry completely.

2. Sand the outside of the box to rough up the surface so that paint will adhere better. Sanding the box wet avoids creating dust in case the existing paint is lead-based.

3. Spray the mailbox with primer and let dry for 15 to 30 minutes.

STARTING THE DESIGN

4. Spray paint some areas of the box blue for the sky and some areas white for the clouds. Be sure to follow all the instructions on the cans of spray products for safety and proper use.

5. Cut simple cloud stencils from manila file folders. After the spray paint dries to the touch (about three hours), position the simple cloud stencils on the mailbox. They can be taped from underneath with drafting tape, which won't pull up the new paint when it's removed. Be sure you use drafting tape (available from office supply stores) and not masking or cellophane tape. A light spray of white along the edge of the stencil will cover a blue area or a light spray of blue will cover a white area and will delineate cloud edges. Let this paint dry for a full 24 hours.

PRINTING THE LEAVES

There are two hints before you set out to print your leaves on your mailbox. Sturdy leaves can be reinked and reused, so you will need to gather fewer items, such as beech, maple, or oak leaves for this project. If you've never nature printed before, or

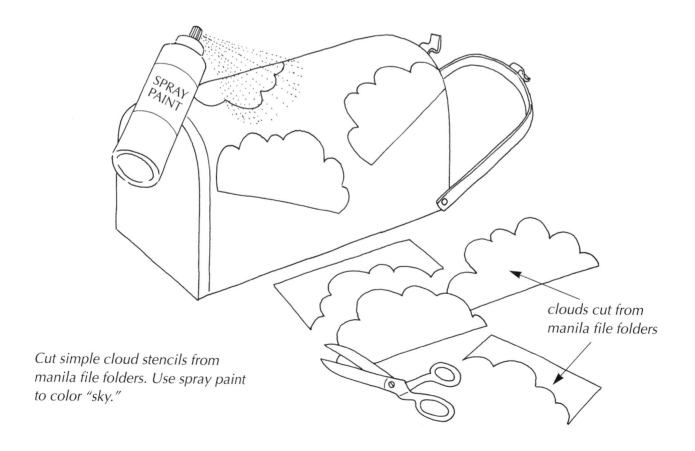

Cut simple cloud stencils from manila file folders. Use spray paint to color "sky."

clouds cut from manila file folders

even if you have, it's always a good idea to make test prints on newsprint to become acquainted with the process before actually printing on your mailbox. Keep in mind that, unlike paper, the mailbox is not an absorbent surface. You may need a heavier application of ink on the leaves when printing the mailbox.

6. When your first painted surface is dry, gather leaves. To create your leaf pattern, tape the leaves to the mailbox and rearrange them until you are satisfied with the design.

7. Prepare the printing inks according to the directions on the packages or tubes. Squeeze out about ¼" blobs of ink in your chosen colors onto your palette and add a few drops of vehicle to each. Mix well using the ink spreaders.

8. Choose your first leaf. Dip the ink applicator into a color. Work the color evenly into the applicator with a dabbing motion on a clean space on the palette, then dab the ink onto part of the leaf. Repeat this process with one or two additional colors until you are satisfied with the result.

9. Pick up the leaf carefully with tweezers, lay it inked side down on the mailbox, and hold it in place with a forefinger. Cover the leaf with a clean piece

Step 6: Arrange and rearrange leaves until you are satisfied with the design.

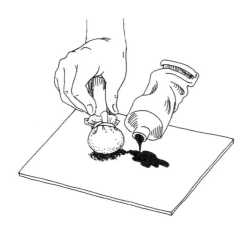

Step 8: Use a dauber to ink your leaves.

Step 9: Be sure to pick up an inked leaf with tweezers only.

of newsprint and press all around it with the heel of your hand and your fingertips. Lift the cover sheet and remove the leaf with tweezers. Repeat this process with as many leaves as you wish until you are satisfied with the design.

10. Allow your mailbox to dry completely. The ink I used took about six days to dry. Apply clear finish as a protective coating.

FINISHING OPTIONS

MOUNTING
This mailbox can be mounted on a standard post for a rural box.

MAINTENANCE
Apply a coat of clear finish once a year to preserve the painted surface of your mailbox.

VARIATION
You may prefer to print garden foliage or wild plants on your mailbox instead of tree leaves. Experiment on paper to find out how a plant prints before printing on your mailbox. Many flowers make beautiful nature prints but are generally more difficult to work with. Practice printing the flowers you plan to use until you achieve success.

More complete information on methods and projects for printing plants and other natural objects can be found in *Nature Printing with Herbs, Fruits & Flowers,* Storey Publishing, 1996.

Victorian Fruit Splendor

MATERIALS

Government-approved, standard-size mailbox

One can ivory satin indoor/outdoor spray enamel — do not use gloss

Acrylic gloss enamel indoor/outdoor craft paints* in the following colors: mauve, white, tan, mossy green, eggshell, light blue, deep blue, dark green, lemon yellow, deep red, peach, chocolate brown, and bright red.

1 can of all-purpose spray adhesive

*I recommend Apple Barrel paints. If you choose another brand, be sure they are made for both indoor and outdoor use.

EQUIPMENT & TOOLS

Nature and herbal stencils
- large grapes
- large cherries
- large plums
- large peaches
- large pears
- bees
- a ladybug

1 artist's liner brush

Stencil brushes in the following sizes: ⅛", ¼", ⅜", and ½"

Foam plates

Paper napkins or paper towels

Cheesecloth, approximately two 1' lengths

Small glass bowl

Plastic gloves

DESIGNED BY SUZIE CARLSON, ART-2-GO BY SUZIE, PERRY, NY

STENCILING WAS ONCE considered a forgotten and little-used art. But in the last decade, it has enjoyed such a burst of popularity that supplies for it are readily available.

The stencil patterns suggested here were selected specifically for their Victorian look and are from the precut nature stencil collection from Art-2-Go By Suzie. These are available at specialty craft and gift shops or see page 119 to order by mail. But if you have a favorite, or want an excuse to try a new pattern or two, feel free to improvise.

Although a knowledge of stenciling is helpful for this project, it is not necessary.

MAILBOX BASE-COAT PREPARATION

1. Follow the directions on the can of spray enamel for the proper use and safety precautions applicable to this product. Spray the mailbox with 2–5 very thin coats of enamel, covering the front, back, top, and sides of the box. Let it dry thoroughly.

2. Paint the flag with two coats of mauve paint. Let it dry thoroughly.

MAILBOX RAGGING

3. Pour about ⅛ cup of mauve paint into a small glass bowl. Add white until the mauve is the next shade lighter. Wearing plastic gloves, dip the cheesecloth into the paint until it is completely soaked. Wring out the cheesecloth until it is damp, not dripping, with paint. Loosely fold and crumple the cloth. Roll the cloth at irregular angles lightly over the surface of the mailbox, applying the lightened mauve sparsely so that the ivory base color still shows through. Continue to roll sparsely, yet evenly, until the whole box is ragged. The mauve paint should be dry almost immediately if it was applied correctly. Be sure it is thoroughly dry before continuing.

4. Mix more white paint with the mauve to achieve a color several shades lighter than the last mixture. Using a fresh piece of cheesecloth, repeat step 3, ragging over the previous ragging to fill in more of the unpainted ivory areas. Let this coat dry thoroughly.

STENCILING PREPARATION AND PLACEMENT

5. In a well-ventilated area, lightly spray the matte side of the stencils with spray adhesive and let it dry. Spray adhesive forms a temporary bond so that you can lay down and pick up the stencils several times.

6. Position each fruit stencil onto one side of the mailbox in the following manner: pears — middle; grapes — lower left; cherries — upper left; peaches — upper middle; plums — lower right; and grapes again at upper right. Make sure each stencil is angled slightly (see illustration below) for a pleasing effect. Stencils should be applied to the opposite side in the same pattern.

7. The front and the back of the mailbox may be stenciled with the grapes singly or in a cluster effect. To achieve a cluster effect, simply stencil the grapes once, cover the upper leaves on the stencil with masking tape, reposition the cluster of berries under the first stenciled image, and stencil again.

8. The bee is stenciled last, and can be applied anywhere there is an empty space. The mailbox featured on page 15 has the bee stenciled on one side of the box, the front opening flap, and also on both sides of the flag.

9. Now you're ready to go. Squeeze about a teaspoon of each color of paint onto a foam plate. Have several paper towels or paper napkins folded and close by. You will be using the smaller size stencil brushes (⅛", ¼") for narrow areas such as the bees and stems. The larger brushes (½", ¾") will be used for areas such as the leaves and fruit bodies. The bee lines are done with a liner brush dipped in paint, then applied at random in short, dotted lines.

STENCILING

10. Start with a dry brush, and keep it that way! This is what is known as the dry brush technique. Holding the brush upright, dip its tip into your first color. You want the paint to be only on the very tips of the brush. Lightly rub the brush in a circular motion on a paper towel or paper napkin. This action works the paint into the brush to distribute it evenly, and removes excess paint. Continue working the brush on the towel until the brush appears almost dry and free of paint. (See example below.)

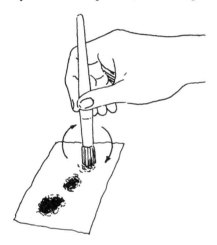

This is very important! Many people are tempted to leave a small amount of paint on their brush, which causes the paint to seep under the stencil edge, giving the finished product a blotchy appearance.

11. Apply the paint to the stencil starting with a counterclockwise swirling motion at the edge of the design. Gradually work the brush into the center. (See example below.) Another way to apply the

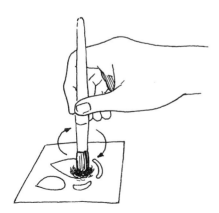

paint is to "pounce" the brush up and down, working from the outer edges of the stencil to the center. (See example below.)

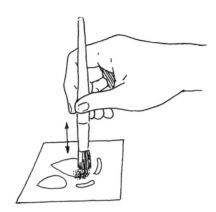

12. When working on this type of surface with this type of paint, the color will need to be built up. To do this, stencil on the color, allow it to dry briefly, then apply more color on top until the ragged background does not show through your stencil. Pouncing is the preferred method for this process because you will be able to apply more paint at one time.

13. Stencil each design in the colors noted in the Stencil Color Guide on page 98. Some colors will be applied as shading or highlight colors only. In this case, the colors are not layered on as much but applied on one side or the middle of the design to give contrast. If you discover that paint is running under the stencil design or is smudged, you have too much paint on your brush or the stencil moved while you were stenciling.

14. Once you are finished, let the paint cure for 24–48 hours before mounting the mailbox outdoors.

STENCIL COLOR GUIDE

Grape leaves	base in dark green, highlight with lemon yellow
Grape stems and tendrils	tan
Grape berries	base in light blue, shade with dark blue
Cherry leaves	dark green
Cherry berries	bright red
Cherry stems	tan
Pear leaves	mossy green, highlight with white
Pear fruit	base of tan, filled in with mossy green, highlighted with eggshell
Peach leaves	mossy green
Peach stems	chocolate brown
Peach fruit	base with dark red, filled in with peach, highlighted with white and lemon yellow
Plum leaves	base of dark green, shaded with tan
Plum stems	chocolate brown
Plum fruit	base of mauve shaded with bright red
Bee	bright red and dark blue
Bee lines	dark blue

FINISHING OPTIONS

MOUNTING
This box would look great mounted on a wrought-iron type post.

MAINTENANCE
No maintenance is necessary except to re-stencil and/or re-rag areas that become chipped, rusty, or damaged.

VARIATIONS
▶ This box can be ragged to match the colors of your residence.
▶ This box can be stenciled without applying a base coat or ragging the surface.
▶ This design can be adapted to any shape or size mailbox.

Boxes for Every Season

LEVEL: EASY TO MODERATE
SEE COLOR PHOTOS ON PAGE 14.

MATERIALS

Three government-approved, standard-size
mailboxes, colors of your choice

Acrylic paints, colors of your choice

Spray varnish or polyurethane

EQUIPMENT & TOOLS

Variety of sizes of pointed and square-tipped
paintbrushes

THERE'S NO NEED to feel limited to just one
mailbox. Let your imagination run wild — create a box for every occasion, or every season.
They're easy to take on and off the post with a
couple of screws. So get out your paintbrushes
to make your own rotating exhibit of mailboxes.

DESIGNING

1. Sketch designs for each box on paper and
modify them until you have settled on one you like.
Transfer the design to the mailbox surface by
redrawing it, cutting out the pieces and tracing them
on the box, or by placing a sheet of carbon paper
face down on the mailbox and tracing over your
design.

2. Paint the design, working from the middle of
the box out so your hand and wrist won't rest in the
wet paint as you work. You may want to work on
one color at a time, letting each color dry for about
30 minutes before applying the next color in order
to avoid smudging. Paint the lighter colors first so

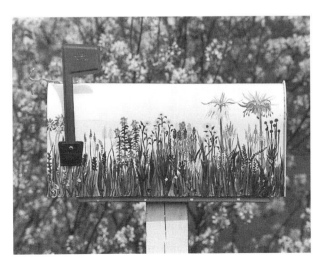

you can cover any "mistakes" with darker, adjoining colors.

3. Once your painting is finished, allow the paint to dry for several days. Finish with a couple coats of spray varnish or polyurethane.

Reproduce your favorite seasonal motif on your mailbox.

FINISHING OPTIONS

MOUNTING

For easy mounting and removal of these boxes, use ¾" screws driven into a horizontal wooden arm extending from the post.

MAINTENANCE

Because you are rotating your mailboxes, your paint jobs should last quite a while. Repaint them if they become chipped, scratched, or rusted. Apply spray varnish or polyurethane as necessary to protect the surface.

VARIATIONS

▶ Incorporate your favorite artistic medium into your personalized design. For example, you can rubber stamp a border around the painted design or add a touch of whimsical charm by gluing on buttons for eyes or fake jewels. Be sure to use weatherproof glue.

▶ If you're not inclined to draw your own design, turn to a source book of traditional designs from quilting, tole painting, or other folk art.

PART II
HOUSE-MOUNTED BOXES

While many of us have our mail delivered to a box on the side of the road, those of us who live in town know the mail carrier who drops our letters into a box attached to the front of the house. These smaller-sized boxes lend themselves to all sorts of opportunities for creative expression.

Some of the projects in the following pages require a bit of woodworking skill while others are designed for the painter. Then there's one just right for anyone who's ever broken a plate or a teacup. Intrigued? Turn the page!

O*versized House-Mounted Box*

LEVEL: MODERATE
SEE COLOR PHOTO ON PAGE 11.

MATERIALS

1 piece 1"x 8" pine or cedar, 12' long, cut into:

> 2 pieces 5½"x11", sides
> 2 pieces, butted side to side, together
>   measuring 9¼"x17", front
> 3 pieces, butted side to side, together
>   measuring 12"x17", back (see illustration
>   on page 103)
> 1 piece approximately 7"x19", top
> 1 piece, 3½"x15¾", bottom

30 9d finishing nails

Hinges

Paint or stain

2 pieces 1" thick wood, each about 10" long, for
    mounting box to house

6 wood screws, for mounting assembly

Wood glue

EQUIPMENT & TOOLS

Clamps

Hammer

Ruler

Sandpaper

Screwdriver

Square

Table saw

DESIGNED BY VINCENT RENE HART ROYCE,
NORTH BENNINGTON, VT
PAINTED BY DEBORAH BALMUTH, WINDSOR, MA

NEED MORE ROOM for your magazines, catalogs, and letters? Then this oversized mailbox will be perfect mounted to the front of your house. This project is fairly simple to construct for someone who is skilled with a table saw.

Once the box is complete, the decorating possibilities are almost endless. The box pictured on page 11 was painted and stamped but you could stencil it, use your nature printing skills, or apply a freehand design of your own creation.

As long as it is not used for mail, this box could be used to hold packages from delivery services that arrive when you're not home.

CUTTING

1. To construct the sides, start with rectangles measuring 5½" x 11". Make your first cut for the pitch of the front. Then, using your square, mark and cut the angle of the roof as shown in the illustrations on the facing page.

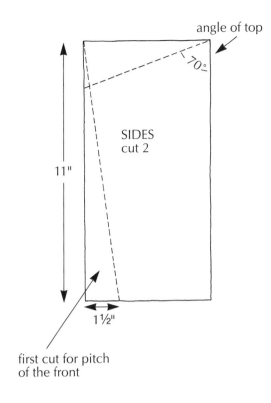

angle of top

70°

SIDES
cut 2

11"

1½"

first cut for pitch
of the front

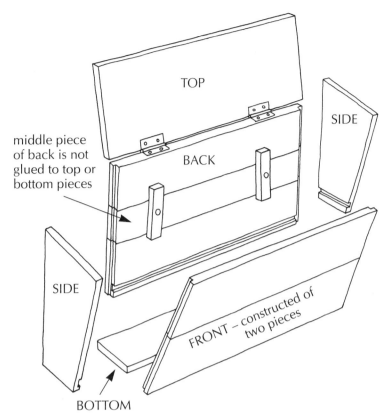

TOP

SIDE

middle piece
of back is not
glued to top or
bottom pieces

BACK

SIDE

FRONT – constructed of
two pieces

BOTTOM

2. The full height of the front and back is made from pieces of 1" x 8" pine that are 17" long . The front is approximately 9¼" x 17" and the back approximately 12" x 17". When you put the back together, use a smaller third piece in the middle of two larger pieces. This middle piece will be attached to the house as part of the mounting assembly. Bevel the top edges of both the front and back to accommodate where the lid will sit. Use the side pieces to set the machine angles. Cut rabbets ⅜" deep in the front and back pieces for a joint with the sides.

3. Cut a ¾"-wide dado ⅜" deep near the bottom inside of the sides and back for the bottom piece.

ASSEMBLING

4. Fit the bottom piece in the dado. Assemble the box with clamps. Drill pilot holes, glue, and then nail the box together. Do not glue or nail the middle back piece, because it will be attached to the house.

5. Secure the hinges to the top of the back piece, then to the lid. The lid's overhang should be over the front of the box.

6. Sand the box, then paint or stain it as desired.

FINISHING

7. The box pictured on page 11 was painted with two coats of nontoxic milk paint available in any crafts supply store. This provides a rustic-looking undercoat for decorative stamping. Allow to dry for at least 24 hours before stamping.

8. To make stamps, draw your designs on cardboard and then cut them out. Trace the cardboard pieces onto a sponge and then cut them out with scissors or an X-Acto knife. Flat, dehydrated sponges work best for this process. Look for them at your craft store. Add water to the sponge if necessary and allow it to dry to full size.

9. To apply sponge prints, pour a small amount of desired color of acrylic paint onto a flat dish or plastic lid. Dip the sponge and test-print it on paper to get the desired paint saturation before applying it to the box. Try printing the back of the box first to test your sponge stamps before applying them to the front and lid.

10. Allow the stamped box to dry for 48 hours before finishing it with acrylic varnish or spray finish for outdoor mounting.

FINISHING OPTIONS

MOUNTING
Secure two vertical spacers 1"x1"x10" to the house about a foot apart and at the height you wish to mount the box. Attach the middle back piece on the two vertical spacers. Screw two retaining swivels onto the inside of the middle back piece, as shown in the illustration below, to hold the mailbox in place.

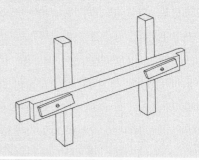

MAINTENANCE
Reapply outdoor varnish or spray finish as needed.

VARIATION
Use stencils, nature printing, or a wood-burning tool to decorate this box. It is versatile enough to accommodate many design possibilities.

Herb-Lover's Garden

LEVEL: EASY

SEE COLOR PHOTO ON PAGE 10.

EQUIPMENT & TOOLS

Nature and herbal stencils:

- small birdhouse on a fence
- small lavender
- small sage
- small chamomile
- small mint
- small watering can
- small nuthatch
- small pine
- small maple leaves
- small log cabin
- small hummingbirds

Low-tack masking tape (available at office supply stores)

One fine-tipped permanent marker, black

Stencil brushes in the following sizes: ⅛", ¼", ⅜"

Paper napkins or paper towels

DESIGNED BY SUZIE CARLSON, ART-2-GO BY SUZIE, PERRY, NY

IF YOU LOVE THE LOOK OF STENCIL, this is the project for you. This is a relatively easy technique to master and it can have outstanding results the first time you try. Check out the color photo for this project for inspiration, then apply your own imagination to create a mailbox like no one else's. The stencils listed are available through Art-2-Go By Suzie and the directions refer to them. They are available at craft shops, or see page 119 to order by mail.

MATERIALS

One residential house-mounted mailbox

One can sage satin indoor/outdoor spray enamel — do not use gloss

Creme stencil paints in the following colors:* snow white, paprika, Wedgwood blue, navy blue, amethyst purple, charcoal green, yellow ochre, hunter green, grape, chocolate

One can all-purpose indoor/outdoor spray polyurethane

*I recommend Delta Stencil Magic Paint Cremes. If you use another brand, try to match the above colors.

BASIC STENCILING INSTRUCTIONS

Start with a dry brush, and keep it that way! This is what is known as the "dry brush" technique.

Holding the brush upright, dip the tip of the brush into the paint. You want the paint only on the very tips of the brush. On paper towels, lightly rub the brush in a circular motion. This serves a dual purpose: You are working the paint into the brush to distribute it evenly, and you are removing excess paint. Continue working the brush on the towel until the brush appears almost dry and free of paint (see illustration A on page 97). This is very important! Many people are tempted to leave even a small amount of paint on their brush, which will cause the paint to seep under the stencil edge, giving a blotchy finished product.

To apply the paint to the stencil, start with a counterclockwise swirling motion at the edge of the design, gradually working into the center (see illustration B on page 97). Another technique is to "pounce" the brush up and down, gradually working from the sides into the center (see illustration C on page 97).

Some colors are applied as shading or highlight colors. These colors are not layered on as much, but rather applied on one side or the middle of the design to give contrast.

If you find that paint is running under the stencil design, or is smudged, then either you have too much paint on your brush, or the stencil moved while you were stenciling.

MAILBOX BASE-COAT PREPARATION

1. Following the directions on the spray enamel can for the proper use and safety precautions of this product. Spray the mailbox with 2–5 very thin coats of sage enamel, covering the outside and inside of the box. Let this paint dry thoroughly.

STENCILING PREPARATION AND PLACEMENT

2. Position your first stencil (the small birdhouse on the fence) on the left side of the mailbox and secure it with a piece of masking tape.

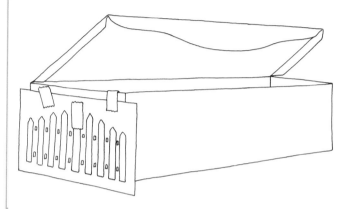

Step 2: *Position your first stencil with low tack masking tape.*

3. You will be using the smaller size stencil brushes (⅛" and ¼") for the narrow areas of each stencil pattern and the larger size (⅜") for the larger areas. Mask off the birdhouse area and stencil only the smaller pickets using the white and paprika paints.

4. Continue stenciling the fence, working from left to right, until you reach the front of the box. Remove the tape from the birdhouse portion of the stencil so that you can use the whole pattern once. Use Wedgwood and navy blue for the birdhouse.

5. Remask the birdhouse and repeat the smaller pickets, stopping at approximately the middle of the mailbox's front.

6. Using amethyst purple and charcoal green, stencil the small lavender, overlapping the pattern several times to build up a full-looking plant.

7. Using hunter green, stencil the sage once, slightly overlapping the lavender for a realistic look.

8. Use hunter green and yellow ochre to stencil the small chamomile next, overlapping it as you did the lavender. You should now have covered the front of the box.

9. Use charcoal green to stencil the mint on the right side of the box, again overlapping.

10. Use grape to stencil the small watering can in front of the mint.

11. Using charcoal green and grape, stencil one hummingbird on the inside of the mailbox cover just under the flap. Add another hummingbird just above the picket fence in the front.

12. On the outside top, stencil the small pine in charcoal green and chocolate, overlapping to create a pine tree branch. Stencil the small nuthatch sitting on the pine using Wedgwood and navy blue.

13. Stencil the log cabin in chocolate, charcoal green, and grape, and the maple leaves in charcoal green, grape, and yellow ochre.

14. Using the permanent marker, create a "chain" for the birdhouse as it hangs from the pine tree branch.

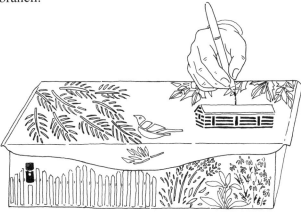

15. Allow the paint to dry thoroughly and cure for 48 hours to a week. Spray with a light coat of polyurethane.

FINISHING OPTIONS

MOUNTING
Follow the mounting instructions included with your mailbox to attach this project properly to your house.

MAINTENANCE
Clean the mailbox occasionally with a damp cloth. Re-stencil or repaint areas that may become chipped, rusty, or damaged.

VARIATIONS
▶ This mailbox can be painted to match or complement the colors of your residence.
▶ This design can be adapted to any shape or size mailbox.

Provençal Whimsey

LEVEL: EASY

SEE COLOR PHOTO ON PAGE 10.

MATERIALS

White enameled house-mounted mailbox (ready to paint)

Small tubes of acrylic fabric paint (with fine point) — colors of your choice in pearl or luster finish

Acrylic paint, color of your choice

Water-resistant clear varnish

EQUIPMENT & TOOLS

Cotton swabs

Paintbrushes

Paper towels

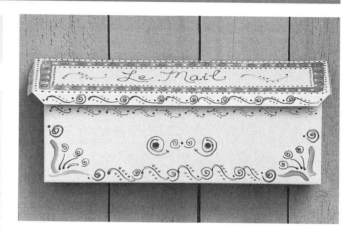

DESIGNED BY LINDA WEISS FREEDLAND,
DELMAR, NY

IF YOU ENJOY PLAYING with design, this is the project for you. Once you're done, there will be no mailbox quite like yours anywhere.

This design is simple and whimsical. The only tools I use are paintbrushes, cotton swabs, and little tubes of fabric paint. Check out the color photo of this project on page 10 as a guide, or be creative and let your imagination soar!

DIRECTIONS

1. Clean the mailbox with a damp cloth. Dry thoroughly.

2. Plan and sketch your design on paper to ensure it will fit on your mailbox. (See top of facing page.)

3. Paint a band of color around the outside of the lid of the mailbox. Let dry.

4. Paint your chosen design on the corners of the box itself. Let dry.

5. Paint the dots around the band of color on the

lid. Be careful not to smudge them. Let dry. Paint swirls inside the band.

6. Using fabric paint tubes, paint the design on the box itself.

7. Once the basic design is done, paint the trim along the edges of the lid and on the sides of the box.

8. The inner portion of the lid can be left unpainted, or you can personalize it with your name, the word "Mail," or whatever suits your fancy.

9. Use water-resistant clear varnish to seal the outside. Let dry completely.

1O. The mailbox is now ready to mount onto your house.

FINISHING OPTIONS

MOUNTING
Follow instructions that come with the mailbox for mounting.

MAINTENANCE
Clean the mailbox with a damp cloth as needed. Touch up the paint as needed.

Privy Mailbox

LEVEL: DIFFICULT
SEE COLOR PHOTO ON PAGE 11.

MATERIALS

1 piece 1" x 4" pine, knot-clear (or D-select), 30" long

1 piece 1" x 6" pine, knot-clear (or D-select), 32" long

2 sturdy wire coat hangers

1 short section of ⅜" dowel or a section cut from round white pencil, for toilet paper roll/door stop

2 pieces of old leather belting, for hinges

15 16-gauge brass brads, ¾"

12 6d box nails

2 round-head wood screws, #8, 1¼", for wire mail holders

1 1" brad for paper roll

Carpenter's waterproof glue

Waterproof stain

EQUIPMENT & TOOLS

Dremel, optional

Drill and drill bits

Hammer

Jigsaw or coping saw

Needle-nose pliers

Sandpaper

Screwdriver

Table saw or radial arm saw

DESIGNED BY EDWARD STOMSKI, ZEE WHAT I ZAW, WELLS, VT

ACCORDING TO SOME PEOPLE, the only reason to have nostalgia for an outdoor privy is indoor plumbing. But this two-holer adds a humorous touch to mail delivery.

This project is somewhat intricate, so you should have some woodworking experience before tackling it.

CUTTING

1. Cut out the pine pieces as shown in the illustrations below. Be sure to save all the scrapwood.

Cutting plan for 1 x 4 pine

← 11½" →	← 12½" →	← 5½" →
SIDE	SIDE	scrap

← 12½" →	← 11½" →

Cutting plan for 1 x 6 pine

← 12½" →	← 11" →	← 8½" →	
BACK	FRONT	ROOF	4½"
		scrap	

2. Drill two toilet holes ½" deep as shown below.

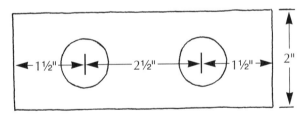

3. Cut the latch bracket and latch bar from the scrap.

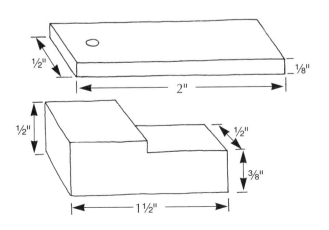

4. Shape and sand all the individual pieces.

ASSEMBLING

5. Glue and nail the side pieces onto the back piece.

6. Glue and nail the toilet-seat section in place, being careful not to nail where the toilet holes are located.

7. If necessary, trim and sand the door to fit in place. Cut a quarter moon out of the door with a jigsaw, and sand it smooth.

8. Stain all the pieces: front, sides, and back. I used Ipswich pine for the roof section and Cuprinol green for the building and door.

9. To simulate planking, make vertical groove lines on the building and door with a table saw, radial arm saw, or Dremel. Set the saw blade to cut ¹⁄₁₆" deep.

10. Using brass brads, nail the leather hinges on the door so that they lay half on the door and half off. Position the hinges 2" from the top and 2" from the bottom of the door.

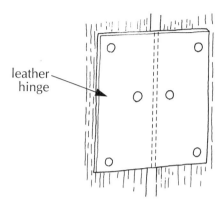

leather hinge

FINISHING

11. Predrill holes for the lock bracket. Glue and then nail the lock bracket halfway down the door.

12. Nail a piece of white-painted dowel or a pencil section with a hole drilled out for a brad inside the door opening, opposite the hinge side, roughly halfway up. This is your roll of toilet paper. It should be set in ¾" from the outside edge of the door so that it stops the door flush with the frame.

13. Glue and then nail the roof onto the sides and back so that it is flush with the back with an even overhang on the sides.

14. Lay the building face up on your workbench to install the door. Make sure you allow for roof clearance so that the door swings open freely. Use brass brads to nail the second half of the hinges to the building.

15. Nail the latch bar to the building with a brass brad.

16. Glue in the block for holding the mail on the inside of the door. Or you can cut a loop from the second coat hanger and place it just inside the door as show in the drawing on page 113.

17. Cut and shape the wire coat hanger for each side of the box as you see it in the illustration below. Use needle-nose pliers to bend eyelets for screws in one end of each piece of the wire. Drill pilot holes for wood screws near the bottom back corner of each side of the mailbox approximately 1" up from the bottom and ⅜" in from back. Attach the wires.

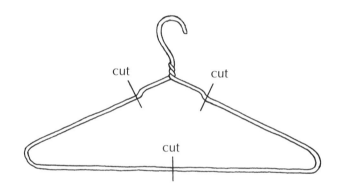

cut   cut

cut

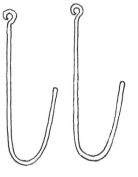

FINISHING OPTIONS

MOUNTING
Mount your privy mailbox to the outside of your house with wood screws through holes in the back of the mailbox.

MAINTENANCE
Restain as needed.

Exploded drawing of Privy Mailbox

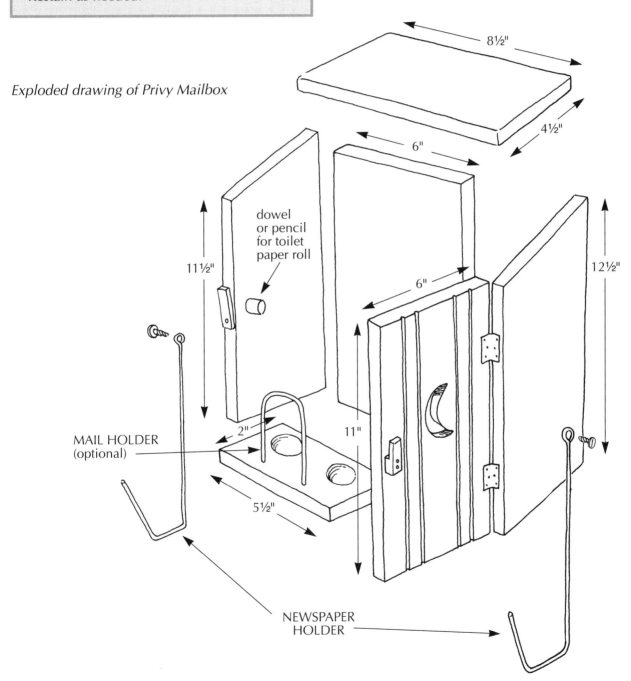

8½"

4½"

6"

dowel
or pencil
for toilet
paper roll

11½"

12½"

6"

11"

MAIL HOLDER
(optional)

2"

5½"

NEWSPAPER
HOLDER

Mosaic Mélange

LEVEL: EASY TO MODERATE
SEE COLOR PHOTO ON PAGE 9.

MATERIALS

Unsanded wall grout

Colorant for grout

Acrylic additive to mix with grout

Ceramic tile adhesive

Dishes, ceramic figures, tiles, buttons, marbles, broken glass (available at tag sales or secondhand shops)

Towel rags

Glue suitable for ceramic and metal

EQUIPMENT & TOOLS

Dremel to grind edges of china

Hammer

Mister with water

Plastic container for mixing grout

Rubber gloves

Safety goggles

Small scraper or butter knife

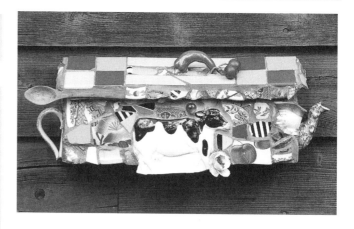

DESIGNED BY MARLENE V. MARSHALL, WEST STOCKBRIDGE, MA

BROKEN ANY DISHES or teacups lately? You can incorporate the pieces into this charming mailbox.

The decorative scheme of this project is limited only by your imagination. It can vary from a simple mosaic made with more or less flat pieces, to a mailbox with a three-dimensional sculptural effect. Just make certain the sculptured pieces are arranged with balance and suitable leverage so that the mailbox opens and closes properly.

PLANNING AND PREPARATION

1. Clean the surface of the mailbox with a damp cloth.

2. Using a hammer, break the dishes, figures, buttons, marbles, and broken glass into manageable sizes. Be sure to wear safety goggles.

3. Choose and arrange the tiles and pieces of broken china into your basic design. Once you have the placement pattern established, glue the pieces into position on the mailbox. Let everything dry until you are sure the glue has set (overnight or longer).

ASSEMBLING

4. In a plastic container, mix the unsanded wall grout with the acrylic hardener, making a mudlike consistency. Using a small scraper or a butter knife, apply the grout between the mosaic pieces. Move the grout around, filling in holes and smoothing out all edges. The grout can be moved up to an hour. A mister of water can remoisten the grout if you need more time.

5. Clean all surfaces you don't want grouted with a damp cloth.

6. With a clean, damp cloth, wipe the surfaces of the mosaic pieces until they are clean. The grout becomes easier to manage as it dries.

7. Mix a small amount of grout and fill in missed spots. Wipe clean as before.

Step 3: Assemble your basic design before gluing on the pieces.

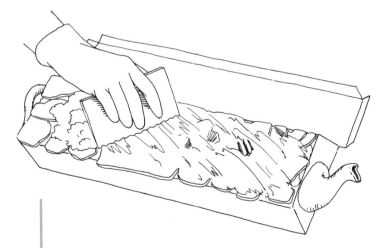

Step 7: Wipe off grout after filling in missed spots.

8. After everything has dried, inspect the surface for rough edges. Use the Dremel to grind them down, eliminating any sharp edges.

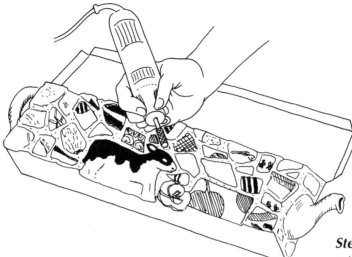

Step 8: Eliminate sharp edges with a Dremel.

9. Polish the china. You will know when all is clean and you are finished.

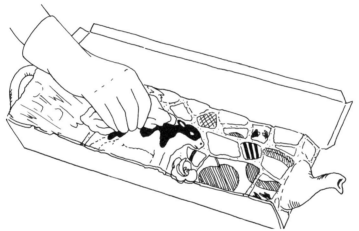

Step 9: Polish the finished surface with a soft cloth.

FINISHING OPTIONS

MOUNTING
Follow the instructions that come with the mailbox to mount it to your house. You might want to use a heavier attachment system (nails or screws) because of the extra weight of the mailbox.

MAINTENANCE
Clean with a damp cloth as needed.

APPENDICES

WHAT IS A BOARD FOOT?

Lumber is usually measured by the board foot (bdf), which is a volume measurement of 144 cubic inches.

Thus a piece of 1-inch board that is 12 inches long and 12 inches wide is exactly 1 board foot.

Similarly, an 8-foot board that is 2 x 6 measures 2 inches times 6 inches times 8 feet divided by 12, or 8 board feet.

KILN-DRIED LUMBER

Nominal Size	Actual size (inches)
1 x 2	¾ x 1½
1 x 3	¾ x 2½
1 x 4	¾ x 3½
1 x 6	¾ x 5½
1 x 8	¾ x 7¼
1 x 10	¾ x 9¼
1 x 12	¾ x 11¼
2 x 4	1½ x 3½
2 x 6	1½ x 5½
2 x 8	1½ x 7¼
2 x 10	1½ x 9¼
2 x 12	1½ x 11¼
4 x 4	3½ x 3½
6 x 6	5½ x 5½
8 x 8	7¼ x 7¼

SELECTING NAILS

This chart shows a wide variety of nail styles, each designed for a specific purpose. Nail sizes are designated by a "d" number. You can use the handy chart to measure your nail in order to determine its d rating. This chart is offered courtesy of Maze Nails (div. of W.H. Maze Company, Peru, IL 61354).

Exterior Nails

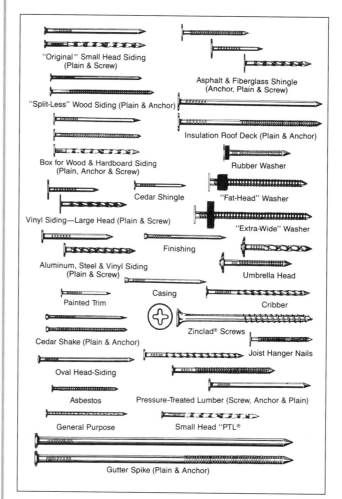

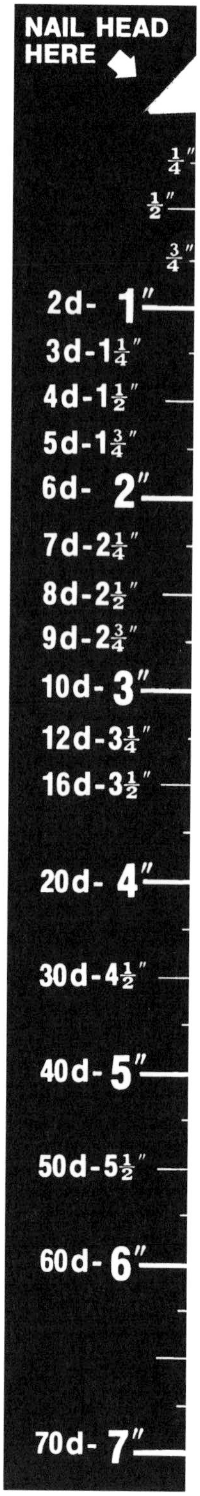

Penny-Inch Nail Chart

2d	1"	9d	2¾"	50d	5½"
3d	1¼"	10d	3"	60d	6"
4d	1½"	12d	3¼"	70d	7"
5d	1¾"	16d	3½"	80d	8"
6d	2"	20d	4"	90d	9"
7d	2¼"	30d	4½"	100d	10"
8d	2½"	40d	5"		

NAIL HEAD HERE

¼"
½"
¾"

2d- 1"
3d-1¼"
4d-1½"
5d-1¾"
6d- 2"
7d-2¼"
8d-2½"
9d-2¾"
10d- 3"
12d-3¼"
16d-3½"
20d- 4"
30d-4½"
40d- 5"
50d-5½"
60d- 6"
70d- 7"

Contributors

*Thanks to the following talented people who designed and built
the mailboxes in this book.*

LAURA DONNELLY BETHMANN, TUCKERTON, NJ

Laura is an accomplished nature artist and author of
Nature Printing with Herbs, Fruits, & Flowers
(Storey Publishing, 1996). She happened upon the
ancient craft of nature printing while painting by a
river one day when she pressed a leaf covered with
a reddish-brown coating to her watercolor paper and
hasn't stopped since. Her work is exhibited in galleries and private collections nationwide.

HAROLD F. BIGELOW, WINCHESTER, NH

Harold retired in 1988 and was occupying his time
in his woodworking shop when his granddaughter
asked if he would chaperone her class on a field trip
to an arts and crafts center. While at the center,
Harold saw Shaker bentwood oval boxes on exhibit
and wondered if he could learn to make them. He
purchased Storey's book ***Simple Gifts*** and started to
learn the Shaker method. He's been making oval
boxes ever since.

SUZIE CARLSON, PERRY, NY

Suzie designs and sells her own line of stencils
through her company, Art-2-Go By Suzie. She
started stencil drawings out of a desire to create
new, one-of-a-kind images. The result is a line of
herbs, bees, bugs, and other nature stencils. To purchase the stencils, write or call Art-2-Go By Suzie,
7859 Schenck Road, Perry, New York, 14530,
(716) 237-5330.

TOM CARPENTER, KINGSTON, ONTARIO

Tom Carpenter is a the author of several building
books, including ***The Basement Book*** (Chapters
Publishing, 1996), and a maker of sturdy mailboxes.

JOE DE JULIO, WATERVLIET, NY

Joe is a longtime woodworker who began making
and selling unique mailboxes in response to cus-
tomer demand. He operates a woodworking business, M & J's Woodcrafters, and has served as
president of the Northeastern Woodworkers
Association.

LINDA WEISS FREEDLAND, DELMAR, NY

Painting was something Linda just dabbled in until
she lost her job in a downsizing move. Left with
"too much time," she turned to painting on boxes.
With the encouragement of her friends, who noticed
her unusual "little boxes," Linda began selling the
boxes in shops and at craft fairs.

ALLYSON HAYES, SARATOGA SPRINGS, NY

Allyson Hayes is a graphic designer and animal
lover.

LISA, KATHERINE, AND JULIA HUNT,
GREAT BARRINGTON, MA

This family of artists includes Lisa, an art teacher at
a private school in Lenox, Massachusetts, and her
two daughters, Katherine and Julia, both of whom
enjoy working in a variety of art media.

DONALD MCAULAY, ERVING, MA

Donald makes and sells rustic furniture in a business he calls Strickly Sticks located in Western
Massachusetts. He learned his craft as a furniture
assembler and refinisher.

MARLENE V. MARSHALL, WEST STOCKBRIDGE, MA

As a result of her work buying and selling antiques, Marlene discovered the folk craft known as pique assiette, or bits and pieces. Intrigued by these memoryware projects, she taught herself the craft. Her pieces are now sold in galleries. Marlene is the author of *Bits & Pieces Mosaics* (Storey Publishing, 1998).

KATHE MOTTOR, EASTHAMPTON, MA

Kathe has been a carpenter and locksmith for many years and now owns her own woodworking business. She recently constructed a series of rustic birdhouses, which she sells at craft shops and fairs.

CARL PHELPS, WILLIAMSTOWN, MA

Carl owns and operates Greenbrier Farm, selling handmade birdhouses and garden accoutrements. He specializes in building pieces from recycled materials.

VINCENT RENE HART ROYCE, NORTH BENNINGTON, VT

Vincent owns and operates a fine woodworking shop in southwestern Vermont. Through his business, Zee What I Zaw, he creates unique birdhouses, sold in craft stores.

EDWARD SMITH, MARSHFIELD, VT

Ed is a fine woodworker who lives in Northern Vermont. His Model A mailbox design is a tribute to this classic car of 1928–31, which he drives the pickup version of daily.

EDWARD STOMSKI, WELLS, VT

Ed has been a carpenter for more than four decades. The Privy Mailbox was adapted from one of his birdhouse designs.

HOW TO ENLARGE A PATTERN

In order to use the patterns provided in this book, you will have to enlarge them to fit your mailbox. Patterns are overlaid with a grid, on which one square equals 1 inch. Photocopy the 1-inch grid provided on the following two pages, then copy the patterns square by square onto this 1-inch grid to create a pattern of the correct size and proportions for your mailbox.

You also may use the enlargement/reduction feature on a photocopier. Experiment with the enlargement until the squares on the finished grid equal 1 inch.

INDEX

Italic page references = Illustrations
Bold page references = Charts

A

Animal patterns, *12,* 34–46
Autumn Sky, *15, 91*
    finishing, 94
    materials, 91
    printing leaves, 92–94, *93*
    starting design, 92, *92*
    surface preparation, 92
    tools/equipment, 91

B

Band saws, 30
Bigelow, Harold, 16
Big Yellow School Bus, *7, 82*
    assembling, 84–85, *83, 84*
    cutting, 83
    finishing, 85
    materials, 82
    painting, 83
    tools/equipment, 82
Bird pattern, *13,* 43–46, *43, 44, 45*
Board foot, 118
Boxes for Every Season, *14, 99, 100*
    designing, 99–100
    finishing, 100
    materials, 99
    tools/equipment, 99
Bright-Eyed Cat, *12, 27, 34*
    cutting, 34, 36
    finishing, 36
    materials, 34
    painting, 36

pattern, *35*
    tools/equipment, 34

C

Cat pattern, *12,* 27, 34–36, *34, 35*
Ceramic, 10
Chop saws, 30–31
Circular saws, 31
Clamps, 28
Customizing mailboxes, 6–8

D

Dremel, 28
Drills, 31
Droopy-Eared Dog, *12, 37*
    cutting, 38
    finishing, 38
    materials, 37
    painting, 38
    pattern, *39*
    tools/equipment, 37

E

Earth-Moving Bulldozer, *8, 86*
    assembling, *87, 88, 89*
    cutting, 87, 89
    finishing, 89–90
    materials, 86
    mounting flag, 89
    painting, 89
    tools/equipment, 86
Equipment. *See* Tools and equipment

F

Fasteners, 27–28
Finishes, 10
Flag mounting, 18, *18*
Flower pots, attaching to posts, *25*
Franklin, Benjamin, 4–5
Funny Finny Fish, *13, 40*
 cutting, 40–41
 finishing, 42
 materials, 40
 painting, 42
 pattern, *41*
 tools/equipment, 40

G

Gloves, rubber, 32
Grout, 10

H

Hammers, 28
Herb-Lover's Garden, *10,* 11, *105*
 base-coat preparation, 106
 finishing, 107
 materials, 105
 stenciling preparation and placement,
  106–7, *106*
 stenciling techniques, 106, *107*
 tools/equipment, 105
Herodotus, 4
House and Planter Mailbox, *6, 65*
 assembling, *66,* 68–69, *68*
 attaching planter boxes, 68, *68*
 finishing, 69
 making house, 66–67
 making planter boxes, 67–68, *67*
 materials, 65
 mounting flag, 69
 tools/equipment, 65
Hummingbird, *13, 43*
 cutting, 43, 45
 finishing, 45–46
 materials, 43
 painting, 45
 pattern, *44, 45*
 tools/equipment, 43

I

Installation, post, 26, *26*

J

Jigsaws, 30

L

Log Cabin, *5,* 27, *55*
 assembling, 56, *56*
 attaching roof and cutting gables, 56–57, *56*
 decorating, 57
 finishing, 58
 materials, 55
 mounting flag, *57,* 58
 shingling roof, 57, *57*
 tools/equipment, 55

M

Masking tape, 31
Materials, selecting, 9–10, 26–28
Measuring tape, 28
Metal snips, 29
Miter box and saw, 29
Model A Ford, *8, 77*
 assembling, 80–81, *80*
 cutting, 78
 finishing, 81
 materials, 77
 painting, 80
 pattern, *78, 79*
 tools/equipment, 77
Mosaic Mélange, *9,* 10, *114*
 assembling, 115–16, *116*
 finishing, 116
 materials, 114
 planning and preparation, 115, *115*
 tools/equipment, 114
Mounting, 18, 23, *23*

N

Nails, 27
 exterior, 118
 penny-inch chart, **118**
Nail set, 29
Nature printing, 11, 92–94, *93*

New England Barn, *7*, 28, *59*
    assembling, 60, *61, 62*
    attaching door, 63
    cutting, 60, 62, *60*
    finishing, 63, *63,* 64
    making windows, 62–63, *62*
    materials, 59
    mounting flag, 64
    painting, 60, 62
    tools/equipment, 59

O

Oversized House-Mounted Box, *11, 102*
    assembling, 103, *103*
    cutting, 102–3
    finishing, 103–4, *104*
    materials, 102
    tools/equipment, 102

P

Paintbrushes, 31
Paints, 10
Patterns, enlarging, 120–22
Pique assiette, 10
Placement and mounting of mailboxes, 18
Planter Mailbox, House and, *6, 65, 66, 67, 68*
    assembling, 68–69
    attaching planter boxes, 68
    finishing, 69
    making house, 66–67
    making planter boxes, 67–68
    materials, 65
    mounting flag, 69
    tools/equipment, 65
Pliers, needle-nose, 29
Postal requirements
    color requirements, 18
    design guidelines, 17
    door regulations, 17–18
    flag mounting, 18, *18*
    markings, 17, *17*
Posts and post designs
    adding an arm, 20
    attaching flower pots to, *25*
    basics, 19

    bracing the arm, 20, *20*
    examples of posts, *21,* 22
    installation, 26, *26*
    lap joints for post arm, *19*
    metal, 23–24, *23*
    mounting, 18, 23, *23*
    pipe, 24, *24*
    platform support for box, 22–23, *22*
    swiveled, *25*
Privy Mailbox, *11, 110*
    assembling, 111–12, *113*
    cutting, 111, *111*
    finishing, 112–13, *112*
    materials, 110
    tools/equipment, 110
Pruning shears, 29
Provençal Whimsey, *10, 108*
    finishing, 109, *109*
    materials, 108
    painting, 108–9
    tools/equipment, 108

R

Radial arm saws, 31
Ragging, 96, *96*
Rugged Bunker Box, *9,* 27, *47*
    cutting and assembling, 47–49, *48*
    finishing, 49
    materials, 47
    mounting flag, 49
    tools/equipment, 47
Rulers, 29
Rural free delivery (RFD), evolution of,
    4–5
Rustic Covered Bridge, *5,* 27, *50*
    assembling, 52
    cutting, 51–52, *51, 52*
    finishing, 53, 54, *53*
    materials, 50
    mounting flag, 54
    tools/equipment, 50

S

Safety goggles, 29
Sanders, 31

Saws
    coping, 28
    hand, 28
    power, 30–31
Scissors, 29
Scrapers, 30
Screwdrivers, 29–30
Screws, 27–28
Scroll saws, 30
Seaside Lighthouse, *4,* 27, *70*
    assembly and decorating, final, *74,*
        75–76, *75*
    cutting and assembling lighthouse, 71–72,
        71
    finishing, 74–75, 76
    making keeper's cottage, 72–73
    materials, 70
    painting, 75
    posts for, 72, *72*
    shingling the roof, 73–74, *73*
    tools/equipment, 70
Seasons, changing, 14–15
    boxes for every season, *14,* 99–100,
        99, 100
Shaker-Style Box, *16*
Squares, 30
Stamping, 11
Stencil brushes, 32
Stenciling, 11, 95, 105
    basic, 106
    color guide, 98
    dry brush technique, 97, *97,* 106
    pouncing, 97, *97,* 106
    preparation and placement, 96, *96,* 106–7,
        106, 107
    ragging, 96, *96*

T
Table saws, 31
Tools and equipment
    hand, 28–30
    power, 30–31
    special, 31–32
Tweezers, 30

U
Utility knives, 30

V
Victorian Fruit Splendor, *15, 95*
    base-coat preparation, 95–96
    finishing, 98
    materials, 95
    ragging, 96, *96*
    stenciling color guide, 98
    stenciling preparation and placement, 96,
        96
    stenciling techniques, 97, *97*
    tools/equipment, 95

W
Wood
    measurements, 118
    paint and finishes for, 10
    patterns, 12–13
    pine, 27
    plywood, 26–27
    selection of, 9, 26–27
    willow, how to identify, 51
Wrenches, 30

X
Xerxes, 4

OTHER STOREY TITLES YOU WILL ENJOY

Birdhouses: 20 Unique Woodworking Projects for Houses and Feeders, by Mark Ramuz.
Includes plans with easy-to-follow illustrations, instructions, materials and tools lists, and ideas for how to finish, decorate, and weatherproof the piece. 128 full-color pages. Paperback. ISBN 0-88266-917-6.

Shortcuts for Accenting Your Garden, by Marianne Binetti.
Hundreds of new, innovative techniques for adding drama and color to the home landscape. Includes line drawings and suppliers list. 192 pages. Paperback. ISBN 0-88266-829-3.

Birdfeeders, Shelters & Baths: Over 25 Complete Step-by-Step Projects for the Weekend Woodworker, by Edward A. Baldwin.
Designs for a wide range of birdfeeders and baths that will attract birds to your backyard all year. 112 pages. Paperback. ISBN 0-88266-623-1.

Be Your Own Home Decorator: Creating the look you love without spending a fortune, by Pauline Guntlow.
Step-by-step instructions for customizing kitchens, baths, bedrooms, and living rooms. Provides unique possibilities for creating an environment that reflects personal style, regardless of cost constraints or ability. 144 pages, with full-color photographs. Paperback. ISBN 0-88266-945-1.

Small House Designs, by Kenneth R. Tremblay, Jr., & Lawrence Von Bamford, editors.
A collection of award-winning, architect-designed plans for houses of 1,250 square feet or less. Judges' comments and designers' concept comments accompany plans for each project. 208 pages, with floor plans and site/elevation renderings. Paperback. ISBN 0-88266-966-4.

Nature Printing with Herbs, Fruits, and Flowers, by Laura Donnelly Bethmann.
Step-by-step instructions for collecting specimens, designing artwork, and painting are provided, accompanied by color photos and illustrations. 96 pages. Hardcover. ISBN 0-88266-929-X.

Homemade:101 Easy-to-Make Things for Your Garden, Home, or Farm, by Ken Braren and Roger Griffith.
Contains complete, easy-to-follow directions that will save you time and money. 176 pages. Paperback. ISBN 0-88266-103-5.

Play Equipment for Kids: Great Projects You Can Build, by Mike Lawrence.
Provides color plans and photos for more than 30 easy-to-build projects for home, patio, and yard. 96 pages. Paperback. ISBN 0-88266-916-8.

These books and other Storey books are available at your bookstore, farm store, garden center, or directly from Storey Publishing, Schoolhouse Road, Pownal, Vermont 05261 or by calling 1-800-441-5700.
www.storey.com